SPORTS POWER

David Sandler

HUMAN KINETICS

Library of Congress Cataloging-in-Publication Data

Sandler, David.
    Sports power / David Sandler.
       p. cm.
    Includes index.
    ISBN 0-7360-5121-X (soft cover)
    1. Athletes--Training of.   2. Physical education and training.   3.
Muscle strength.   I. Title.
    GV711.5.S26 2005
    613.7'11--dc22

                                            2004020075

ISBN: 0-7360-5121-X

TCP

Acquisitions Editor: Ed McNeely; **Developmental Editor:** Jennifer L. Walker; **Assistant Editors:** Mandy Maiden and Michelle M. Rivera; **Copyeditor:** Annette Pierce; **Proofreader:** Coree Clark; **Indexer:** Bobbi Swanson; **Permission Manager:** Toni Harte; **Graphic Designer:** Robert Reuther; **Graphic Artist:** Sandra Meier; **Photo Manager:** Dan Wendt; **Cover Designer:** Keith Blomberg; **Photographer (cover):** Tom Roberts; **Photographers (interior):** David Sandler and Steve Bamel unless otherwise noted; **Art Manager and Illustrator:** Kareema McLendon; **Printer:** Versa Press

Human Kinetics books are available at special discounts for bulk purchase. Special editions or book excerpts can also be created to specification. For details, contact the Special Sales Manager at Human Kinetics.

Printed in the United States of America

10   9   8   7   6   5   4   3   2   1

Human Kinetics
Web site: www.HumanKinetics.com

United States: Human Kinetics
P.O. Box 5076
Champaign, IL 61825-5076
800-747-4457
e-mail: humank@hkusa.com

Canada: Human Kinetics
475 Devonshire Road Unit 100
Windsor, ON N8Y 2L5
800-465-7301 (in Canada only)
e-mail: orders@hkcanada.com

Europe: Human Kinetics
107 Bradford Road
Stanningley
Leeds LS28 6AT, United Kingdom
+44 (0) 113 255 5665
e-mail: hk@hkeurope.com

Australia: Human Kinetics
57A Price Avenue
Lower Mitcham, South Australia 5062
08 8277 1555
e-mail: liaw@hkaustralia.com

New Zealand: Human Kinetics
Division of Sports Distributors NZ Ltd.
P.O. Box 300 226 Albany
North Shore City
Auckland
0064 9 448 1207
e-mail: blairc@hknewz.com

To my parents, Joyce and Steve, and to Edina
for supporting and believing in my ability
to reach my dreams.

CONTENTS

ACKNOWLEDGMENTS

To keep this brief would be impossible as so many have helped mold my career and given me the insight to develop this book. First and foremost, I would like to thank my best friends and partners, Steve Bamel and Ed McNeely, not only for their help and contributions to this book, but for the rare friendship and their support and loyalty for all my crazy ideas. Their passion for our common goal is unmatched.

I would like to thank my mentors, Dr. Richard Lopez and Dr. Joseph Signorile, for their endless hours spent making me a better teacher and practitioner. It is rare to find such a passionate, inspiring teacher and friend in an advisor, let alone two. Additionally, I would like to acknowledge Dr. Robert Wolff for giving me the opportunity to teach and develop the field of strength and conditioning at such a high level.

My career would never have "taken off" without the help of Dale Hulett, John Philbin, and Tommy Moffitt—three of the finest strength coaches in the business. Thanks for your wisdom and being the role models that you are.

I would like to extend a special thanks to two lifetime friends and training partners during my powerlifting career: Mike Thor and Craig Stevenson.

Without a doubt, I must thank my new family at Arnold Classic Productions, Jim Lorimer and his staff, for giving me such a great opportunity. And in particular Dave Ryan for helping get things started. Also, I would like to extend special thanks to Jim Stoppani and the crew at *Muscle and Fitness* for many exciting opportunities and future plans. Also, I cannot forget Bruno Pauletto and Power Systems for believing in and supporting StrengthPro.

I would also like to thank Mike Barnes, Keith Cinea, Doug Lentz, and Virginia Meier at the NSCA for acknowledging my capabilities and showing me their true respect for the field of strength and conditioning.

Thanks to the HK staff (Jennifer and Mandy) for their patience and hard work on this project. And also a special thanks to Debbie Sandelman for her editing efforts and putting up with me during this whole process.

Again, there are so many people to acknowledge in being part of my career such as Jim Bell, Gary Scott, Jose Antonio, and Ken Kinakin. I am sure I have left out some of you; however, it was not intentional.

And finally, I would like to thank my students and all the athletes I have coached. Without you, my desire to find the best training methods and the guts and inspiration of this book would have never begun.

INTRODUCTION

When asked to describe a powerful athlete, most people think of someone large and hulk-like, yet many other body types can create tremendous power. A lanky high jumper requires a great deal of power to hurl his body eight feet up and over the crossbar, and a tiny gymnast displays amazing power in a tumbling pass. Power, as physics defines it, is the rate at which work is performed. Or for the purposes of this book, power is the optimal combination of speed and strength. In fact, the faster you can move an object (which may be your own body), the more powerful you will be. Therefore, it is your job to determine how much power your sport requires, then incorporate the appropriate amount of power training into your program.

Whether your sport entails long endurance activity or extremely short bursts, power and the ability to be explosive can improve your performance at every level. The ability to break away from an opponent, jump to block a shot, or stop and cut back at a moment's notice makes the difference between winning and losing. And superior athletes have found ways to perform these movements better than their opponents.

To achieve superior athleticism, you must execute fundamental skills flaw-lessly. The ability to perform flawlessly is built through training. And like any well-built structure, sound support mechanisms form the basis of longevity. The same is true of training for sports success. A long athletic career must be built on the four pillars of power.

Pillar one: Physics of power Because the human body and its ability to move are governed by the same forces acting on our planet, it is essential to understand how physics plays a role in sports. When asked about physics, most people have a hazy recollection of Sir Isaac Newton's laws of motion. And although this book is not intended to validate Newton, Einstein, or any other great visionary, understanding a few basic concepts will help you develop the proper exercise prescription for improving power. Nearly 400 years later we are still examining Newton's work and applying his principles to movement and developing better equipment to help the athlete. It is now time to apply these laws to training.

Pillar two: Power of physiology Physics alone is not the only challenge in developing power. You must develop specific motor patterns and supply energy at a rate fast enough to allow your body to perform the given task. The human brain, and in particular the motor cortex, becomes the critical link between this pattern and athletic success.

The human brain is like a giant sponge. Over its lifetime it continually collects bits of information and stores them in a unique filing system. Rather than organizing this information alphabetically, for example, the human brain builds a database based on how often you need the information. The more you use a piece of information, the easier it is to retrieve, and the better you get at retrieving it. The opposite is true for information you do not use often. The instructions necessary for performing a task are permanently etched in your brain after you have performed it once, but if you don't use the information or perform the skill, your brain stores the instructions a little deeper. That is why the more you practice a skill, the better you get at it. In the case of developing explosive power, the more you work on strength and speed and the more you combine the two through practice, the more powerful you will become. In this book, we learn how to build and use the perfect filing system—the ability to call upon specific muscles in the proper sequence as fast as possible.

Pillar three: Philosophy of power   To be powerful is more than exhibiting tremendous strength and speed, it is also being unmatchable and unconquerable and able to stay at the top of your game. This requires a philosophy that will prevail in individual matches and over the course of a long career, a philosophy built on respect and admiration for your competitors as well as the desire to work hard day in and day out. This philosophy is essential to developing sports power. To become more powerful, you must work at 100 percent effort every single repetition. Anything less will not produce the desired results.

This philosophy comes with drawbacks, however. The harder you work, the faster you fatigue, which reduces the volume of your workout. Secondly, you are limited by the weakest link, be it within yourself or a teammate. And most important, you limit yourself if you do not believe you are capable of improving. So to ensure success in both your training and on-field performance you must not only work hard, but you must believe in yourself and your teammates.

Pillar four: Psychology of power   Only a few athletes achieve the greatness to make the all-star team, set world records, or make the hall of fame. Great athletes work hard, but more important, great athletes believe that they must continue to work hard to be the best. Being powerful in this respect is having mental and moral vigor along with the willingness to continue at all costs. Not only does the psychologically powerful athlete possess physical might, but he or she also possesses a superior capacity to endure. How else can you explain the last-second heroics found in sports? Time and time again we are blown away by the feats of athletes who appear to have nothing left. You have no doubt heard sports announcers say, "That performance was all about sheer determination."

Philosophy is a state of being or a disposition, but psychology is something much deeper. In many cases, the ability to believe is far more powerful than the ability to do. Although the term *90 percent mental* may be an exaggeration, it does say a lot about the importance of being into whatever it is you are doing. However, even if you believe, you are still limited by the role that physics and physiology play in the outcome. Whether or not you believe in yourself, you must still address the motor pathway issue to produce the force and speed necessary to be powerful.

Success is built one training day at a time. To unleash your inner power is to declare that you are all powerful in all aspects. The four pillars are the keys to unlocking your power. As you work through the training stages in this book, remember the pillars with every rep, every set, and every exercise. Mentally, you must be willing to put in the effort during these workouts and practices to maximize results. Practices and workouts that train power are as valuable as any other form of training and should be approached as if they were game time every time!

1

Determining Your Power Profile

To gain an edge over your competitors you need to be more powerful. But what exactly is power, and how do you develop it effectively? To truly understand power and its impact on sport and training, you should understand a few fundamental concepts of physics—specifically Newtonian physics. That's where we begin.

Newton's first law states that an object in motion stays in motion, unless an outside force acts upon it. Scientifically, this refers to inertia, or the fact that an object wishes to remain as it is, and therefore, moving it requires a force greater than its own. The larger and heavier the object, the greater its inertia and thus more force is required to overcome it. In terms of contact sports, the larger and heavier your opponents, the more force you need to overcome them.

Newton's second law suggests that the force necessary to overcome an object's inertia is directly related to the object's mass and its acceleration. In the case of the human body, if you want to jump, you must apply enough force to overcome your body weight and the acceleration of gravity, which pulls you back to the earth.

Finally, the most well known is Newton's third law: For every action, there is an equal and opposite reaction. Therefore, if you want to jump up, you must exert force downward through your feet equal to the amount of force necessary to overcome gravity and your weight. To jump higher, you need to produce more force. The trick in sport is to determine how much force you need and when you need to produce it.

So how do these laws help us describe power? Really, only Newton's second law helps with the mathematical calculation of power; however, the first and third laws will help us choose specific drills to enhance power.

$$P = W / t$$

Mathematically speaking, power (P) refers to the rate (t) at which work (W) is performed. In layperson's terms, it is how fast you can produce force. In sport performance terms, it is how fast you can move your body, move an opponent, or move an implement such as a racket. The more slowly you perform these movements, the more likely you'll produce negative results.

$$W = F \times D$$

Work is defined as the amount of force (F) produced over a specific distance (D). The greater the distance the object or body must travel or the greater the force necessary to move the object or both, the greater the amount of work that must be performed. For example, lifting a 50-pound (22.68 kilograms) sack of potatoes onto a two-foot-high (.61 meters) shelf requires less work than lifting that same sack to a four-foot-high (1.22 meters) shelf. But here is something interesting: You accomplish the same amount of work lifting a 25-pound (11.34 kilograms) sack to a four-foot-high shelf as lifting a 50-pound sack to a two-foot-high shelf. Understanding what's happening in each example is extremely important when developing a training program. Given that the same workload is being accomplished, which training method would you employ? Don't answer that yet; instead, read on.

$$P = (F \times D) / t$$

Here is where it gets interesting. I'd be willing to bet that most people can lift a 25-pound sack much quicker than a 50-pound sack. The question to ask then is, "How much faster can the 25-pound sack be lifted?" Let's use an example that most people are probably familiar with—the bench press. If you were to take a 100-pound (45.36 kilograms) bar and move it to arms' length at two feet in one second or a 200-pound (90.72 kilograms) bar to arms' length but it took three seconds, which produced more power? You got it, the lighter load! Imagine that 200 pounds was your single best one repetition maximum. One hundred pounds would be 50 percent of that maximum weight. It is possible that a lighter weight produces more power!

$$2 \text{ ft} \times 100 \text{ lbs} = 200 \text{ ft lbs}$$
$$2 \text{ ft} \times 200 \text{ lbs} = 400 \text{ ft lbs} = \text{more work}$$
$$200 \text{ ft lbs} / 1 \text{ sec} = 200 \text{ ft lbs} / \text{sec} = \text{more power}$$
$$400 \text{ ft lbs} / 3 \text{ sec} = 133 \text{ ft lbs} / \text{sec}$$

Ready to answer the question about which training method to use, the 25-pound or 50-pound load? Hang on, and read a little more.

$$P = F \times V$$

In general, the heavier the object, the more slowly it moves. Plus, the heavier the object, the greater its inertia, and the greater the force required to move it. Therefore, there is a cost associated with producing force: velocity (V). Force and velocity are inversely related (figure 1.1). To increase velocity, you must lighten the load. And when you increase force, you must move more slowly. To understand this concept more clearly, think of picking up or curling a dumbbell with very heavy weight—it does not move fast at all and the heavier the weight you choose, the slower you move it. Now pick up a very light weight and try to move it as fast as possible—it moves much faster. So light weights can be moved

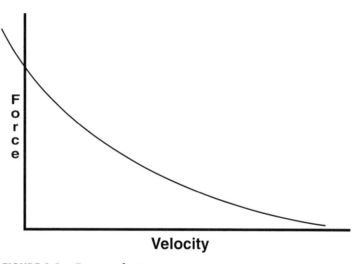

FIGURE 1.1 *Force–velocity curve.*

faster. The cost issue is where this relates to sports where speed is essential. If you constantly practice moving objects slowly (lifting heavy weights) then you are not typically improving velocity. And while strength may be increasing, the speed at which you can exert that force does not, and thus the speed at which you exert force (rate of doing as the above equation suggested) does not improve if you just lift heavy all the time (again, this supports the need for more than just strength training to produce power). Somewhere between super heavy and super fast is the optimal way to produce power. This is seen by looking at the force–velocity curve.

$$V = D \, / \, t \text{ from the equation}$$
$$P = (F \times D) \, / \, t$$

Power is the optimal combination of force and velocity. Because it is impossible for an athlete to produce maximum velocity and maximum force at the same time, movement will always be limited.

Optimal power is said to occur between 30 and 60 percent of the maximum force attainable. This means that an athlete will produce his or her maximal power at a load that is between 30 and 60 percent of his or her maximal one-repetition effort (figure 1.2). However, it is not always desirable to produce

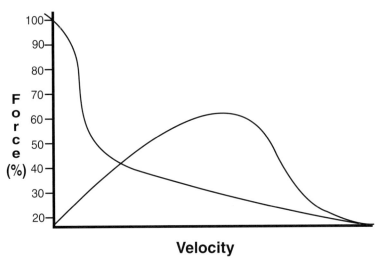

FIGURE 1.2 *Power curve.*

maximal power. For example, when throwing an off-speed pitch or passing the soccer ball to a teammate accuracy is most important. Therefore, power training should be tailored to meet the demands of the sport and the position. In later chapters, you learn how to combine the best of both worlds. In later chapters, you will learn how to achieve maximal power and gain the most from both speed and strength training.

So, is it better to be stronger, faster, or more powerful? When lifting a heavy object, overall strength may be best. While sprinting, it matters not how strong you are, but how fast you can get to the finish line. In a sport like the shot put, the weight of the shot is predetermined; therefore, you need the combination of speed and strength. And in soccer, you may need speed, strength, and power at different times in the game. Figure 1.3 illustrates the needs of three different athletes.

In sports it's important that you don't create extra work for yourself, because the amount of work you must produce directly affects your ability to sustain activity. In other words, work causes fatigue. Therefore, to reduce the negative effect that work has on your body, you may benefit by decreasing the time it takes to perform a task. This is not to say that you can reduce the required work entirely (you still must run 100 meters to win the race), but you can reduce the amount of time it takes to complete it. Your particular sport may dictate the direct interaction of force and the distance that must be covered. In that case, the only variable you can reduce is time. But where appropriate, reducing the force necessary is the ideal solution. A note should be made here that, in true physics, there is a difference between speed and velocity, as well as force and strength.

Force and velocity compete against one another when lifting weights and propelling your body. A heavier athlete tends to move more slowly than a lighter

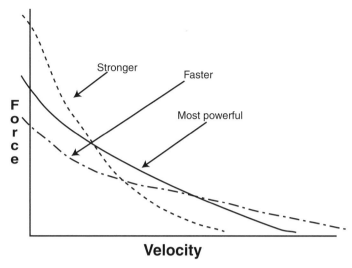

FIGURE 1.3 *Who's the better athlete?*

one, and a heavier weight tends to move more slowly. Often the cost of being a larger athlete is foregoing speed; however, that is not to say that all large athletes are slow. Speed training improves the ability to move a large object more quickly, and thus improves overall power.

So, when two athletes are competing, does the heavier athlete always win? You have the choice of increasing your strength to overcome your opponent's inertia or increasing velocity to overpower him. Remember, in sport you merely need to make your opponent vulnerable. Therefore, you must plan to train power specific to the requirements of the sport.

IDENTIFYING YOUR POWER NEEDS

Science defines power as the rate at which work is performed. This means that the faster you perform work, the more powerful you are. Combine that speed with moving an object, such as an implement, body, or some other form of resistance, over a certain distance and you create power. Although the science is useful, as an athlete you define power in terms of your work—the sports you play, the results in competition, and the workouts you create—and work to achieve the optimal combination of speed and strength.

Sport scientists are on a constant quest to define power, too. They seek to develop new training techniques, better equipment, and innovative training tools to extract power from athletes, pushing athletes to achieve the incredible records that we see today. In other words, sport scientists work to produce maximal power techniques to achieve the sporting dream. To achieve this dream, we need to incorporate a bit of all three of these definitions (science, athlete, and the sport scientist) and that's what we turn to next. I call this combined definition the *power profile*. Creating a power profile can be compared to a physician diagnosing an ailment. A strength and conditioning coach will take time to assess your current strengths and your areas of weakness through a battery of strength tests. The strength coach will examine the results and then develop the proper exercise prescription based on the diagnosis. To make a proper diagnosis it is necessary to examine not only the athlete, but also the needs of the sport. Therefore, the typical diagnosis–prescription model used in everyday exercise prescription must be modified for each athlete. In this chapter you learn to use specially designed prescriptive strength tools to diagnose your current abilities and from there, develop a power profile for you and your sport.

To identify the needs of your sport, you must look at how you and your team play. For example, certain movements can be classified as powerful, strong, fast, or endurance. To classify these movements accurately, one must understand the biomechanical factors that govern speed and strength. Although power may not predominate your sport, some sort of power training will be beneficial. To decide which power exercises are right for you, you must analyze the speed–strength continuum (figure 1.4).

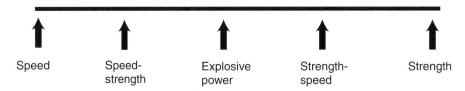

FIGURE 1.4 *Speed–strength continuum.*

Pure Speed

At one end of the continuum is speed. Speed can be defined as the ability to rapidly recruit muscle fibers. True speed is the combination of antagonistic muscle groups working together, not simultaneously, but in sequence. To be a fast runner you not only need a strong, quick push-off, but you also must rapidly cycle the leg through each phase of the stride. To do this, you must train the hips, legs, and butt, as well as the upper body and torso. Take this one step further to the act of throwing a baseball more than 90 miles per hour and see the speed of the arm in rotation reach more than 7,000 degrees per second. Speed not only refers to how fast you run, but also how fast your body parts can move to drive a golf ball 300 yards, hit a homerun, or slap a puck past the goalie. Often when we think of speed, we imagine a sprinter burning up the track, but in today's sporting world of tennis serves over 150 miles per hour, sprint speed touches on only a small component of the athletic world. Fortunately, speed training has come a long way from training only sprints.

Sports that fall at the speed end of the continuum include most throwing activities; swinging a racket, golf club, or baseball bat; and kicking and punching movements. The sports that use these movements are easily identified, but may

A sport such as badminton falls near the speed end of the speed–strength continuum because an athlete's muscles must fire rapidly to swing the racket.

not be considered pure speed sports. To help you determine the needs for your sport, you can look up the position of your particular sport and its movements on the speed–strength continuum.

All speed sports require the muscles to fire rapidly and sequentially to produce tremendous body segment and joint speed. Additionally, most high-speed movements end with a follow-through movement that slows the motion. Without this follow-through you would throw your arm out of the socket, or your arm would slam into your body at high speed. Explosive activity needs follow-through. Movements that require the follow-through to slow the body down serve as another marker for determining high-speed activities and should be a major factor in determining the speed-training requirements of your sport. And finally, most high-speed sports release an implement or contact an object with an implement. Based on these criteria, you can see that running is not necessarily a high-speed activity. It uses no implement and because the movement is continuous, there is no follow-through after contact. And finally, the joints do not move nearly as quickly as those used for throwing and hitting.

Recall that power is located in the middle of the continuum and that it is the optimal combination of speed and strength. The heavier an object (such as your body), the more strength you need to move it. Thus, you begin to move toward power and away from pure speed. The speed training strategy is simple: Movement should be as rapid as possible. Whether the exercise uses resistance or not, the movement must be rapid. And this emphasis on speed dictates light resistance.

Pure Strength

At the other end of the continuum is the ability to call every muscle fiber into play to produce force. At the pure-strength end, speed is almost nonexistent. As long as the object in question moves, speed is not a factor. A strong athlete has a distinct advantage in injury reduction and overall durability. In sports like powerlifting, where overcoming inertia is the key element, strength is champion. Other sports that belong in this category include strongman events and activities featuring other feats of strength.

Strength is a major factor in exercises such as the deadlift where an athlete must overcome inertia.

Although often confused with power, strength may be the most easily identifiable aspect along the speed–strength continuum. The contractile force generated by a muscle or group of muscles determines strength. A simple, or single-joint, strength move is an arm curl (contraction of the biceps to move the arm at the elbow), and a multijoint movement uses several muscles working together to create movement around several joints (like performing the squat movement). If your sport requires you to move heavy objects, strength is a major requirement. However, these sports are limited to the very obvious lifting-type activities.

Pure-strength training is best done with very heavy weight and low repetitions. An easy way to determine whether you are in the strength zone is by how fast the resistance travels. In true strength training, speed is not a factor. The weight should be heavy enough that the movement is slow. Strength training serves as a base for explosive activity. Most athletes incorporate some form of strength training at some point in their program.

The ability of a muscle to exert force is the measure by which some people incorrectly gauge sports performance. For example, in the weight room, the person who bench presses the most weight is considered the superior athlete. However, power, not strength, determines athletic superiority.

Remember that speed and strength are not determined solely by genetics. Although in both cases heredity certainly plays a big role, speed and strength can be trained.

Pure Power

Pure power sits in the middle of the continuum and is the combination of speed and strength. Its production is continual and produced as needed. Power is constantly required whenever there is movement. For example, getting out of a chair requires some speed and some strength—strength to lift the weight of the body and speed to fight gravity. Now, try to get out of a chair very slowly and see what happens. To get out of your chair you must use power. Although you only need enough speed and strength to lift your body, if you choose to get up slowly (meaning more strength, less speed), it is quite difficult. Why? There are two reasons. First, you need to overcome the effect of gravity (meaning you have to move at least as fast as the gravitational pull against you), and second, your legs alone do not provide an effective lever system for producing strength against the line of force (through the feet). Since most of your body weight is not directly over the feet, you must move the body into position to produce force, and this cannot be done slowly or movement would look very robotic. To combat this problem you must produce power. Sports that fit the pure-power category include those that propel the body through the air such as jumping or throwing heavy objects, such as the shot put or hammer. Typically, a sport that requires vertical velocity to propel the body into the air requires both speed and strength. This optimal combination of speed and strength helps the body develop enough force and velocity to overcome the inertial effects of gravity. The long jump, high jump, and jumping to block shots in basketball or initiate kills in volleyball qualify as high-power activities.

© Empics

Jumping to initiate kills in volleyball is a high-power activity that places the sport on the pure-power end of the speed–strength continuum.

One of the major characteristics that differentiates the pure-power athlete from others is the rapid shift of the body from position to position. This is usually achieved by rapidly performing an eccentric movement prior to concentric movement known as prestretching (and explained later in the book). Again, when combating gravity or trying to become airborne, power is the essential ingredient.

Speed-Strength and Strength-Speed

At one end of the power continuum is speed, and at the other is strength. Because optimal power is developed as a combination of speed and strength, a true power athlete falls somewhere in the middle. But now take a look at a sport where you must move an object, for example moving your body to block an opponent or get across the court, or even moving an opponent. To classify sports that are mixed, such as tennis, soccer, sprinting, hockey, football, and many of the common team sports, there are two additional categories: speed-strength and strength-speed. Separating these categories from the nearer category (meaning speed-strength from speed and strength-speed from strength) is more difficult since many sports overlap definitions in more then one category. These two categories cover about 70 percent of individual sports and almost all team sports to some extent. Although it's true that each sport exhibits attributes from each of the categories, being able to clearly identify which category your sport falls into is a great asset when determining your overall power training strategy.

Speed-strength Sports that move the body across the ground are classified as speed-strength. Running in soccer and tennis and sprinting events displays the dominant movement patterns associated with this category. Sports where the feet

FROM THOUGHT TO EXECUTION

Cut right, dodge the punch, jump to block the shot—all regular tasks associated with a particular sport. Why is it that some athletes just do it better, quicker, and with more grace? It's like a riding a bicycle. Remember the first time? Not so easy, but I bet that even those of you that have not gotten on a bike in more than 20 years could do it, no problem! How many of you could ride a unicycle, though? The human brain is like giant sponge. It continually, over its lifetime, collects millions of bits of information. During the information gathering, it builds its very unique filing system. Rather than organizing things alphabetically, however, it builds a database based on frequency of need. In other words, the more you use it, the better you get at it while the opposite is true when you do not use it. So why are you still able to ride a bike after all those years? Unlike our filing cabinets, the brain never really throws anything away, it just stores it somewhere for later use. The skill set necessary to do a task has been permanently etched in the brain, but often it is put aside. The more you practice, the better you get at the skill set and the faster or more efficiently you call upon a skill. Just like a well-organized filing cabinet; it's always easier to find something when you know where to look!

The more tabs you place in your filing cabinet and the more specific you get in your classification system, the faster and more productive you become. The more you specifically train each component of your skill set, and the more you practice the entire skill, the better you become at it. In the case for developing explosive power, the more you work on strength and speed, and the more you combine the two with the practice of the particular skills, the more powerful you will become. Thus you will build the perfect filing system—the ability to call upon the specific muscles necessary in the specific sequence, as fast as possible.

Training then is more an issue of figuring out what is needed rather than just getting stronger or faster! Again, being explosive is the optimal combination of speed and strength. Developing the optimal pathway to call upon strength and speed is the key to developing optimal power.

Training specifically refines the filing system by forcing the nerve tissue to "rewire" the signal process so that it can be done quicker. In the case of producing more strength, it rewires the system so that more muscle fibers are called into the activity. This process is known as recruitment. Superior athletes possess a superior ability to recruit muscle fibers to perform a task—whether it is for speed, strength, or power. When you first perform a new movement, it takes time to perfect it (riding the bicycle for the first time). As you practice a skill, your brain and all of its components refine your movement skills, engrain the specific motor pattern, and recruit the correct muscle fibers in the optimal sequence to perform a coordinated movement. Developing power then is a matter of speeding up this sequence and calling more muscle fibers up to perform the task. Thus power can be trained, and is not just gifted.

predominantly remain in contact with the ground or close to it and have regular movement patterns such as forward, backward, shuffling, and low-level jumps are best situated in this category (note that kicking and serving are pure speed).

Strength-speed   Simply put, these are the rough, tough sports where physical contact presides. Football, hockey, rugby, and wrestling fall into this category. Certainly these sports require pure-strength actions and even pure-speed or speed-strength movements. But the most important factor for classifying this group is that contact requires slightly more strength than the pure-power classification. Moving heavy objects or people with enough velocity as seen in tackling, checking, and rucking determines this power profile.

DEVELOPING A POWER PROFILE FOR YOUR SPORT

To help locate your sport on the continuum, use table 1.1 as a guideline in determining your sport's power requirement. Keep in mind that several variables, such as coaching philosophy and team strengths and weaknesses, can determine where your sport sits. You also must take into consideration the level of play. Certainly a high school team will have a different power profile than a professional team, and likewise women will have a different profile than men. For example, studies have shown that the average tennis point in a men's game lasts about two racket contacts only. A point in a women's game averages three or four. With double the racket contacts and speed of shots, women's games are slightly different from men's games.

But what do you do if your sport is not listed in table 1.1? Find the sport most similar to yours and use the same guidelines. However, because several factors affect classification, you must understand how to determine the power contribution of your sport. You can do this by using the following five-step approach:

1. View recordings of athletes competing at your skill level. They should be of the same gender. You can record it yourself, or view something already recorded. The tape should show the bulk of the game and not just the star athletes.

2. Examine the video for the major characteristics outlined by each subcategory of the speed–strength continuum by counting the number of times the athlete jumps or how much the athlete runs (by time or distance).

3. Determine what percentage of the sport's movements correspond to each category of the speed–strength continuum as displayed in table 1.1.

4. Based on the needs of your sport, build your power profile. This will vary by position in team sports, by level of play, and by gender. For sports where the course or terrain changes, such as tennis on clay or grass, and where the game style changes with it, you may need to build several different mini power profiles.

Table 1.1 Power Requirements of Various Sports

Sport	Speed	Speed-strength	Explosive power	Strength-speed	Strength
Powerlifting	0	0	0	5	95
Weightlifting	0	0	10	50	40
Judo	0	10	10	60	20
Karate	30	60	10	0	0
Boxing	30	50	20	0	0
Wrestling	0	10	10	60	20
Shot put	0	10	50	40	0
Golf	95	5	0	0	0
Rowing	0	15	20	60	5
Baseball	45	30	20	5	0
Tennis	40	40	20	0	0
Squash	50	40	10	0	0
Racquetball	35	35	30	0	0
Rugby	5	15	20	40	20
Football	0	20	40	30	10
Sprint cycling	25	60	15	0	0
Soccer	20	70	10	0	0
Field hockey	15	60	15	10	0
Hammer throw	5	60	25	10	0
Ice hockey	0	30	30	40	0
Lacrosse	15	25	25	35	0
Alpine skiing	0	20	55	15	10
Basketball	5	60	25	10	0
Volleyball	25	40	35	0	0
Jumping max effort	0	20	80	0	0
Sprinting	10	70	20	0	0
Throwing max effort	95	5	0	0	0
Distance running	10	80	10	0	0
Swim sprints	5	70	20	5	0
Swim distance	15	80	5	0	0

This table represents the relative percent of time that the sport would exhibit movement patterns associated with each of the speed–strength continuum categories. Note: This does not mean that a basketball player should not pure-strength train (because it has a 0). It just suggests that very few, if any, movements are pure strength. Also, this chart represents most of the players on each sport team; however, there are exceptions such as a goalie (mostly pure power/explosive strength), or quarterback that throws often (pure speed).

5. Stick with your plan. Do not second-guess yourself midway through your training program. You must stay on track if you want to see results. If you work hard enough, results will occur, and modifications in your training prescription will be necessary, especially as you become faster, stronger, and more powerful.

Now that you've located your sport on the continuum, what is the best training method for your particular sport? In the next chapter, we get one step closer to finding out so that you can begin improving your power—assessing your power profile.

2

Assessing Your Power Profile

Fitness testing has become a regular part of athletics. Testing can range from simple sprint tests for time to much more complex laboratory tests that measure blood, pH, oxygen consumption, recovery ability, and hormone levels. The results of these tests are often used to rank players against known norms or other players on their team. Although testing is a valuable gauge, a good testing program provides more than just numbers for comparison purposes. It breaks down your performance into its elements, allowing you to determine specific physical components that need to be improved so that your training program can focus on those areas that will provide the greatest training benefit. This is particularly important when assessing a complex variable like power.

As you saw in the previous chapter, optimal sport-specific power combines appropriate amounts of speed and strength. To develop an individualized power profile you need to measure strength, speed, and power. The tests that you select and their relative importance depend on the demands of your sport and where it falls on the speed–strength continuum. Table 2.1 shows the tests for each of the groups on the continuum.

Once testing is complete, test results have many uses. They can be used to compare athletes with one another or against national norms within a sport.

Table 2.1 Preferred Tests for Assessing Current Strength, Speed, and Power

Speed	Speed-strength	Explosive power	Strength-speed	Strength
Velocity on serve of throw	Standing 40, flying 40	Vertical jump, running vertical jump	Loaded vertical jump, bench press throw, seated shot put	1RM tests for large multijoint movements like squat, bench press, or power clean
Leg turnover bike test	Leg turnover bike test	Number of clap push-ups in 10 sec	1RM tests	Loaded vertical jump
Estimated strength test	Estimated strength test	10-20 yd sprints	Standing 40, flying 40	Bench press throw

They can be used to assess strengths and weaknesses and help establish specific training protocols. But most important, tests provide a starting place. To quote my doctoral advisor, Dr. Joseph Signorile, associate professor at the University of Miami, "How do you know where to go if you do not know where you are?" With this no-nonsense approach in mind, let's get started.

POWER TESTING

Power testing can be broken into two categories: general and specific. Both offer clues to your power production abilities and weaknesses.

General Sport Tests

With equipment costing tens of thousands to hundreds of thousands of dollars, assessing true power can be expensive. However, a few easy-to-administer tests can give you a general idea of overall body power. General power tests determine how the lower body moves against gravity, something done in most sports.

Jump tests are general tests of power that are simple to perform, require little equipment, and are safe for almost everyone. Jump testing involves static jumps without a preload and countermovement jumps where the athlete dips or preloads before jumping.

Static vertical jump (SVJ) The static vertical jump (SVJ) measures concentric lower-body power. To perform the static jump you need gym chalk, a tape measure, and a high wall.

First, chalk the middle finger of one hand. Then, stand perpendicular to the wall so that the chalked hand is closest to the wall. Reach as high as possible and place a mark on the wall. Now, step six to eight inches from the wall and squat down as far as you can while keeping the feet flat on the floor. Without dipping downward (*a*), jump as high as you can, swinging the arms, and reaching as high as possible to place a second mark on the wall (*b*). Repeat for three to five trials. Measure the distance between the reaching height and maximum jump height to the nearest quarter of an inch.

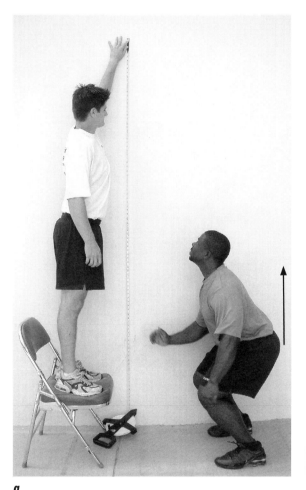

a
b

Countermovement vertical jump (CVJ) The countermovement vertical jump (CVJ), when compared to the static vertical jump, assesses the contribution of the stretch-shortening cycle to power performance. The setup for the CVJ is similar to that of the SVJ.

The CVJ starts from a standing position. Next, rapidly dip (*a*), and jump as high as possible, swinging the arms and reaching as high as possible to place a mark on the wall (*b*). Repeat this sequence for three to five trials. Measure the distance between the reaching height and the maximum jump height.

a   *b*

Another version of this jump, the running vertical jump (RVJ), uses a running start. To perform this jump, you need a Vertec or other jump measurement device.

First, start three to five steps from the device, run up to the Vertec, and perform a two-legged jump, swinging the arms and reaching as high as possible. Repeat this jump for three to five trials. Record the best jump. Subtract this score from a reaching height to calculate vertical-jump height.

While the running jump-version results can be constructive, the CVJ is the jump most people are familiar with and the one they refer to when discussing how high they can jump. Table 2.2 shows the average vertical jump height for a variety of athletic groups, along with averages for other athletic tests. Use this table to determine whether your jump power is adequate for your sport. If your sport is not in the table, find another sport in the same group from the speed–strength continuum and use those values.

Table 2.2 *Vertical Jump, T-Test, 40-Yd Sprint, Hexagon Test, and 300-Yd Shuttle Descriptive Data* for Various Groups of Athletes*

Sport/position	Vertical jump in.	Vertical jump cm	T-test sec	40-yd sprint sec	Hexagon test sec	300-yd shuttle sec
NCAA Division I college football split ends, strong safetys, offensive and defensive backs	31.5	80		4.6–4.7		<59.0
NCAA Division I college football wide receivers and outside linebackers	31	79		4.6–4.7		<59.0
NCAA Division I college football linebackers, tight ends, safetys	29.5	75		4.8–4.9		<61.0
College basketball players (men)	27–29	69–74	8.9			
NCAA Division I college football quarterbacks	28.5	72		4.8–4.9		
NCAA Division I college football defensive tackles	28	71		4.9–5.1		<65.0
NCAA Division I college basketball players (men)	28	71				
NCAA Division I college football offensive guards	27	69		5.1		<65.0
Competitive college athletes (men)	25–25.5	64–65	10.0	5.0	12.3	
NCAA Division I college football offensive tackles	25–26	64–66		5.4		<65.0
Recreational college athletes (men)	24	61	10.5	5.0	12.3	
High school football backs and receivers	24	61		5.2		
College baseball players (men)	23	58	9.2			
College tennis players (men)	23	58	9.4			

(continued)

Table 2.2 (continued)

Sport/position	Vertical jump in.	Vertical jump cm	T-test sec	40-yd sprint sec	Hexagon test sec	300-yd shuttle sec
High school football linebackers and tight ends	22	56		5.4		
College football players	21	53		5.35		
College basketball players (women)	21	53	9.9			
17-year old boys	20	51				
High school football linemen	20	51		4.9–5.6		
NCAA Division II college basketball guards (women)	19	48				
NCAA Division II college basketball forwards (women)	18	46				
NCAA Division II college basketball centers (women)	17.5	44				
Sedentary college students (men)	16–20.5	41–52	11.1	5.0	14.2	
18- to 34-year-old men	16	41				
Competitive college athletes (women)	16–18.5	41–47	10.8	5.5–5.96	12.9	
College tennis players (women)	15	38	11.1			
Recreational college athletes (women)	15–15.5	38–39	12.5	5.8	13.2	
Sedentary college students (women)	8–14	20–36	13.5	6.4	14.3	
17-year-old girls	13	33				
18- to 34-year-old women	8	20				

*The values listed are either means or 50th percentiles (medians). There was considerable variation in sample size among the groups tested. Thus, the data should be regarded as only descriptive, not normative.

Reprinted, by permission, from E. Harman, J. Garhammer, C. Pandorf, 2000, Administration, scoring, and interpretation of selected tests. In *Essentials of strength training and conditioning*, 2nd ed., edited by T.R. Baechle & R.W. Earle (Champaign, IL: Human Kinetics), 310.

The SVJ can be combined with the CVJ to determine the effectiveness of the stretch-shortening cycle. Your CVJ should be at least 15 percent higher than your SVJ. If your difference is less than 15 percent, you need to focus on plyometric training, covered in chapter 7. A difference of greater than 15 percent indicates that you use the stretch-shortening cycle efficiently.

The RVJ can be used to further test your ability to use the stretch-shortening cycle. Your RVJ should be higher than your SVJ and CVJ. The RVJ tests your ability to quickly change your momentum and direct power in the opposite direction. If your RVJ is less than your CVJ, your ability to change direction under load needs work by increasing eccentric strength in the lower body. Note here that concentric refers to the positive portion of the movement or typically the contraction of the major muscles to produce the movement. Eccentric refers to the negative portion of the movement or the lengthening of the muscles. Eccentric activity that precedes the concentric movement for added force is known as the prestretch and significantly increases force output.

Specific Sport Tests

Assessing the power of a specific limb action such as punching or kicking and assessing the power of movements similar to those found in a particular sport are considered specific tests. Many coaches employ tests that mimic sport movements, or they create scenarios that are specific to the sport. Finding tables that allow you to compare these test results against normal values can be difficult; however, these tests are great for comparing power within your own team.

Loaded jump tests   Loaded jumping allows you to assess power throughout the force–velocity curve and is a great test for monitoring specific power development across the speed–strength continuum. Loaded jumps can be performed on a CORMAX squat machine (*a* and *b*), Smith machine, or using a weighted vest. The CORMAX device allows heavier loads and is better for athletes at the strength end of the speed–strength continuum because it provides a more complete assessment of the entire spectrum. The Smith machine allows heavy loads,

a

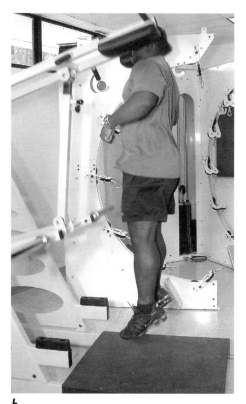

b

but the forces experienced during landing increase the risk of injury, making it a second choice to the CORMAX.

The weighted vest is more convenient but only allows testing at light- to moderate-force levels. You need a vest that can be loaded with at least 40 pounds. Test procedures are the same as for the CVJ. Increase weight by 10 pounds for each trial up to the weight limit of the vest. Regardless of the loaded jumping method you choose, the data interpretation procedures are the same.

Draw a graph of jump height versus weight (see the example in figure 2.1). Plotting follow-up graphs allows you to determine if your lower-body power production is increasing appropriately according to the speed–strength continuum. For example, those at the pure-strength end of the continuum should see greater jump heights with higher loads, those at the speed end should see improvement in jump heights with small or no load, and those in the middle of the continuum should see improvement with light to moderate loads (figure 2.2).

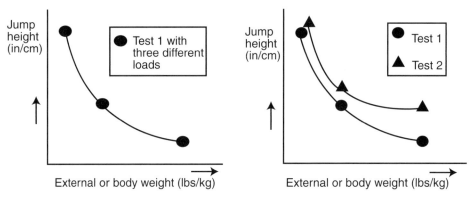

FIGURE 2.1   Graph of jump height versus jump weight.

FIGURE 2.2   Graph of two tests of jump height versus jump weight.

This graph can use jump height in inches or centimeters and can be measured against the athlete's body weight, external weight, or both. Be consistent so you can plot the improvement. Weight can be measured in pounds or kilograms.

After training for strength or strength-speed, the athlete sees the greatest improvements in jump height at the heavy load end of the graph.

Jump testing when the arms are used measures full-body power. A well-timed and explosive arm swing can account for 15 to 20 percent of jump height. In order to isolate the lower body, the jumps described earlier can be used, but hold the hands above the head during the jump. Removing the arm swing results in jump heights about 15 percent lower than those using the arms. If you do not see this difference, insufficient shoulder power may be limiting your jump performance.

Static lateral jump (SLJ) Lateral jumps assess lower-body power in a lateral direction. You need masking or duct tape and a tape measure. Just like vertical jumps, these tests can be done with one leg or two and can use the arms or not.

First, place a piece of tape on the floor. Stand on one foot with the hands behind the back, foot on the tape. Bend the leg to about 90 degrees, swing the other leg, and without dipping, jump sideways as far as possible. Repeat for three to five jumps in each direction.

Countermovement lateral jump (CLJ) Setup is the same as in the SLJ. From a standing position, dip and swing the opposite leg to the side (*a*), jumping as far as possible (*b*). Repeat for three to five jumps in each direction.

a   *b*

Interpret the data for these tests in the same way as the SVJ and CVJ; you should see a 15-percent difference between the two. If not, you need to focus on explosive plyometric training.

Upper-Body Throw Tests

Most tests of power and speed are for the lower body and usually include jumping activities. However, many athletes need to assess and develop power in the upper body. Existing tests are limited; however, research to develop new equipment is being conducted.

Bench press throw   The bench press throw, like the loaded vertical jumps, allows you to assess concentric muscle power throughout most of the speed–strength continuum. The athlete's one-repetition maximum (1RM) determines the starting weight and the increment for increasing weight. Determine your 1RM on the same Smith machine you will use for the throw test, one or two days before performing the bench press throw.

To perform this test you need a flat utility bench, a set of Olympic-style free weights, a Smith machine, a tape measure, and a video camera. Next, mount a tape measure on or next to the Smith machine so that you can see how high the bar travels when it is thrown. Set up the video camera perpendicular to the Smith machine so that it can clearly capture the numbers on the tape measure. Lie on the bench and set the safety stops so that the bar will stop just before it touches the chest (*a*). Bring the empty bar to the safety stops where it will rest until the command to lift. With the video camera running, drive the weight up explosively, throwing it as high as possible (*b*). Repeat this procedure, increasing by 10 percent of your 1RM until the weight can no longer leave the hands. Rest at least 60 seconds between attempts.

Once all attempts are completed, analyze the video. Using the frame-advance mode on the camera or video recorder, determine the height of the bar at the top of each throw. Subtract the bar's starting height to determine the throw height. Plot these values on a height versus weight graph.

a

b

A variety of Smith machines are on the market. A linear machine on bearings is the best type for this test. Counterbalanced Smith machines allow a light enough weight for most athletes, but if you can bench press more than 325 pounds, you can use the version that is not counterbalanced.

An alternative to this exercise is the drop bench press throw. The drop bench press throw measures the contribution of the stretch-shortening cycle to upper-body power. Equipment and setup are identical to the bench press throw, with the addition of one or two spotters. Instead of starting at the chest, the bar is held about 10 inches above the athlete's outstretched arms and is dropped into his hands following a ready command. The athlete catches the bar, quickly decelerates it, and throws it for maximum height. Analyze the video in the manner described for the bench press throw.

Seated shot put throw   The seated shot put throw measures upper-body power. An eight-pound shot, tape measure, and a wall or chair are needed for this test.

Sit with the back flat holding the shot at the shoulder with forearms parallel to the ground (*a*). Throw the shot as far as possible for three to five trials (*b*).

a

b

Measure the distance to the nearest quarter-inch. Note: A practice session the day before the test helps new athletes determine the optimum throw angle and decreases the effect of skill on the variation among a team's test results.

Lower-Body Speed Tests

Speed is the change in an object's position divided by the time it takes to accomplish the change. Running speed is a complex variable that depends on stride length and stride rate and becomes further complicated when change of direction is added into the mix. One of the objectives of speed testing is to determine the underlying physical attributes that may limit speed.

Standing-40 or flying-40 acceleration The 40-yard dash is widely used to evaluate an athlete's speed; however, if your sport has a specific accepted timed sprint distance then use that accepted measure. Although it is a relatively simple test, several factors affect its accuracy: the accuracy of the course, the timers, and the running surface. First and foremost, the distance must be measured accurately. A variation of a single yard will significantly affect an athlete's time. Performing this test on a football field should alleviate this problem. For a flying-40 the athlete runs an additional 10 yards before timing the 40-yard distance.

A straight 40-yard dash starts with the athlete in his normal sport starting position; however, a football player starts in a three-point stance. Start timing when the athlete makes his first move, and end when part of the body crosses the finish line (generally speaking, without light timing it would be head or chest).

The 40-yard dash is a good indicator of acceleration. In such a short distance the faster the initial acceleration, the faster the time will be. To measure the athlete's speed after the initial acceleration, use the flying-40 test. Mark a 50-yard course. The first 10 yards serve as the initial acceleration period and are not timed. As soon as the athlete covers 10 yards, start timing. And just like the 40-yard dash, stop when the athlete crosses the finish line.

Athletes moving from the high school to the college game often find that they appear to run much more slowly. Although their college times are slower, they aren't actually running more slowly. They're just experiencing the difference between hand and automatic timing. Most high school coaches time sprints with stopwatches. Hand timing presents several problems. Scouts, coaches, and other talent evaluators are fairly accurate with the old-fashioned system of stopwatches. However, unless you are very well practiced, I recommend investing in a light timing system, which is the most accurate way to time the 40-yard dash. This system uses two beams of light: When the athlete moves and breaks the first beam, the clock starts, and when the athlete crosses the finish line and breaks the second beam, the clock stops.

The last thing to consider in the 40-yard test is the running surface. Times are different on a track, artificial turf, natural grass, or a synthetic-grass field. Organizations, including the NFL, have developed tables to convert 40-yard dash times by surface.

Stride length test   This test is used to measure the athlete's ability to accelerate from a stopped position. To perform this test you will need a field or track marked off in a 20-meter section, a stopwatch, and two coaches.

The athlete will perform six, 20-meter sprints from a standing start. In between each sprint the athlete will take as much time as he needs for full recovery. The first coach will record the time it takes to complete 10 strides by starting the stopwatch on the first foot strike and stopping it on the last foot strike. The second coach will measure the distance covered by the 10 strides. The coach should compare the results of the tests with previous results.

Pro agility   The pro-agility test measures an athlete's agility, or ability to change direction rapidly, and acceleration. Measure off a line 10 yards long and mark perpendicular lines at either end and in the middle. Begin by straddling the center-line with feet shoulder-width apart in the stance you use for your sport. On the "go" signal, run as fast as you can to the line at the right end. After touching the right line, turn and sprint 10 yards back to the line at the left end. After you have reached the left line, turn and sprint through the centerline. Timing begins at the initial movement toward the right line and ends once you have passed through the centerline the final time.

Leg turnover bike   Most coaches prefer running speed tests to bike tests, citing the fact that athletes don't ride bikes during a game. Although it is true that bikes are not used in a game; testing is not always about simulating a sport. Tests also measure underlying physical abilities. Leg turnover rate is a key factor in determining running speed, and although stride rate can be tested while running, moving your body weight during a running test affects maximum turnover rate. Bike testing is a powerful speed assessment tool that measures leg turnover without load, giving a true measure of leg speed and indicating the athlete's potential for speed development.

A Monark brand bike ergometer is best, but any bike with adjustable resistance will suffice. The Monark bike has a distinct advantage because both its wheel diameter and pedal revolution have been set so that each pedal revolution causes the wheel to spin six meters, which makes calculating distance and speed easy. Set the seat height so that the leg is slightly bent when seated on the bike with the pedal at the bottom of the stroke. The load, or resistance, on the bike should be set as low as possible. Heavier loads result in greater power but can affect the leg turnover rate.

To begin, set up a video camera perpendicular to the bike and zoom in on the pedal so that you have a clear view of the foot and the pedal. After a three- to five-minute warm-up on the bike, turn on the camera, and accelerate to half speed. On the "go" command, pedal as quickly as possible for 15 seconds. At the end of the test, review the videotape, counting the number of pedal revolutions in each five-second period. Count to the nearest quarter revolution. If your camera doesn't have a time-based counter, you can use the frame-by-frame advance to calculate the elapsed time. Most cameras shoot at 32 frames per second; therefore, counting the number of pedal revolutions in 160 frames gives you the same value as a five-second count. Table 2.3 shows the peak five-second turnover rate you need to shoot for in each of the groupings along the continuum. There are relatively inexpensive revolution counters that attach to bike wheels that can be purchased at local bike shops. It may be worth investing in counters if you plan on doing many bicycle tests.

If you have not achieved this goal from the table and you are in a sport that requires running speed, your ability to generate leg turnover is holding you back. Quickness and agility drills from chapter 6 will help you improve.

Table 2.3 Bike Leg Turnover Test

	Speed	Speed-strength	Explosive power	Strength-speed	Strength
Men	14.25–16.5	13.75–15.0	13.0–14.25	12.0–13.5	9.0–11.5
Women	14.0–16.0	13.0–14.5	11.0–12.75	11.25–12.75	9.0–11.0

The numbers in this table represent peak five-second turnover rates.

Upper-Body Speed Tests

In sports like baseball, tennis, and golf, implement speed is important to athletes and coaches. For example, increasing club head speed usually results in a longer drive. Unfortunately, measuring implement speed is virtually impossible without specialized equipment. Radar guns, timing systems, and accelerometers can give very accurate readings but are not available to most people. Video analysis is more accessible, but it is limited because most cameras only shoot at 28 to 32 frames per second, making the measurement accurate to only 0.03 seconds, which is a large margin of error for very high-speed activities.

Recall from our physics lesson in chapter 1 that to determine speed or power, we need to divide distance by time. Therefore, measuring high-speed actions over short distances is difficult. Accuracy is limited by a short distance that may be insufficient to actually time the object. And if we can time it, our expertise with a stopwatch over that short distance will be the limiting factor. Calculating distance, mass, and acceleration when propelling a heavy object is easier.

Strength Tests

Strength can be classified as either absolute or relative. Absolute strength represents the maximum amount of weight you can lift one time. Large people tend to have greater absolute strength than small people because they carry more muscle mass. Relative strength is the maximum amount of weight you can lift one time in relation to your body weight. Relative strength is more important to athletes who must accelerate their own body weight vertically, laterally, or linearly.

The amount of weight you carry affects your speed during sport. If speed is an important component of your sport, then increasing absolute strength through weight gain is of no benefit if the added weight slows you down. Increasing relative strength makes it easier to accelerate your body because you have increased your strength without increasing your body weight.

There are two types of strength testing. Maximal strength testing, often called 1RM, measures the maximum amount of weight you can lift one time. Submaximal repetition testing uses a lighter weight, more repetition, and a formula to estimate maximum strength. The results of strength testing can be expressed in absolute terms or divided by body weight to estimate relative strength. Although you can use any free-weight or machine exercise for strength testing, it consists of three or four major multijoint exercises that assess full-body strength. Table 2.4 *a* and *b* provide strength-to-weight goals for men and women for common exercises for each of the groupings on the speed–strength continuum.

Table 2.4a Strength-to-Weight Goals for Men

	Speed	Speed-strength	Explosive power	Strength-speed	Strength
Squat	1.1–1.4	1.4–1.6	1.6–2.0	2.2–2.5	2.5+
Bench press	1.1–1.4	1.4–1.6	1.8–2.0	2.1–2.4	2.6+
Deadlift	1.1–1.4	1.4–1.6	1.8–2.0	2.1–2.4	2.6+

The numbers in this table represent percentages of body weight.

Table 2.4b Strength-to-Weight Goals for Women

	Speed	Speed-strength	Explosive power	Strength-speed	Strength
Squat	0.8–1.0	1.0–1.3	1.4–1.7	1.8–2.0	2.0+
Bench press	0.8–1.0	1.0–1.3	1.4–1.7	1.8–2.0	2.0+
Deadlift	0.8–1.0	1.0–1.3	1.4–1.7	1.8–2.0	2.0+

The numbers in this table represent percentages of body weight.

1RM tests   Maximum strength testing (1RM testing) can be a time-consuming process. It normally takes between 20 and 40 minutes per exercise for a true max test. The procedure starts with a warm-up with a light weight you can easily handle for 5 to 10 reps. Rest two minutes. Increase the weight by 10 to 20 percent and do a second warm-up of three to five reps. Rest two minutes again. Increase the weight by another 10 to 20 percent, and perform a final warm-up of two or three reps. This time, rest three to four minutes. Increase the load by 5 to 10 percent, and try one repetition. Rest three to four minutes, again. If the last attempt was successful, increase the weight by 5 percent and try another repetition. If it was not successful, decrease the weight by 2.5 to 5 percent and try again. Repeat this process until only one repetition can be performed with proper technique (*a* and *b*). Always rest three to four minutes between attempts at this point.

a

b

Ideally, the 1RM will be determined within five sets of finishing the warm-up. If it takes longer than this, fatigue may affect the accuracy of the test. Normally, this type of testing is accurate to within 5 percent of the true 1RM.

Estimated tests   An alternative to 1RM testing is the estimated test. The estimated test may be a more efficient use of your time. These tests use formulas
to predict maximum strength. In most cases these tests are as accurate as the
1RM test. They are less accurate for athletes who train very close to their max
for long periods at a time.

Like the 1RM test, the procedure starts with a warm-up with a light weight
you can easily handle for 5 to 10 reps. Rest two minutes. Increase the weight
by 10 to 20 percent and do as many reps as possible. You should reach failure
between 2 and 10 reps.

For sports that do not have a large strength application, performing multiple
repetitions and predicting your maximal weight may be all you need. The following formulas will help you predict your strength maximum (1RM). In chapter 9,
you will see how predicting maximums are used in programs.

Upper body rep max predictor

$$\text{Weight used for reps} \times \left(\frac{1}{(1 - [\text{Reps made} \times .025])} \right)$$

Lower body rep max predictor

$$\text{Weight used for reps} \times \left(\frac{1}{(1 - [\text{Reps made} \times .035])} \right)$$

Always remember that in using these tests or creating your own battery of tests,
tests should be designed for the needs of your sport. With your power profile
in hand, you're ready to move forward and build a strength base that will form
the foundation for power training. The next chapter shows you how.

3

Building a Base

Before developing speed and strength that can be transferred to power, it is necessary to build a strong base—establish a foundation for developing power. Much like building a house, the foundation is the key to the longevity of the entire structure. Strength provides that base on which power and subsequent sports success will be founded.

To build the house, you must have a plan. An architect creates a step-by-step process for contractors to follow. These plans, or blueprints, guide the builder as he or she works on the house. For training, your blueprint is your program, and that program must be complete, detailed, and mapped out if you are to achieve sports success. How can you create a power program without understanding the process for increasing power? You can't. Therefore, before we set out to build the base, add the walls, and finish the roof, we need to focus on the overall plan.

PROGRAM DESIGN

Choosing the correct exercises and applying the proper progression are important for reaching your goals and minimizing your setbacks. Granted, for the average person looking to gain fitness, almost any exercise combination will provide results. However, designing a program to improve competitive sports performance becomes more difficult.

In chapter 1 we saw in the speed–strength continuum how training must zero in on the specific adaptation we are trying to achieve. In this chapter we focus on building the base that will prepare your body to handle the rigors of the power training program. Therefore, before beginning sport-specific training, you must map out the following information in your blueprints.

Goals of the program   In choosing an appropriate strategy for maximizing your training potential it is important to determine the true reason for your need for training. Helping you produce power is the ultimate goal of this book. Therefore, your training goal is to prepare your body to endure explosive, ballistic exercise. The immediate goal is to develop a strength base that will allow you to apply a speed element to it. Meeting this goal establishes the framework for correctly choosing the exercises.

Strength levels   Remember, however, that ultimate strength is only one aspect of sports performance, especially in sports where fine-motor skills are needed. Categorize your need for strength based on the needs of your sport. A simple scale such as that in figure 3.1 will help you determine where you stand and, ultimately, how much base building you need.

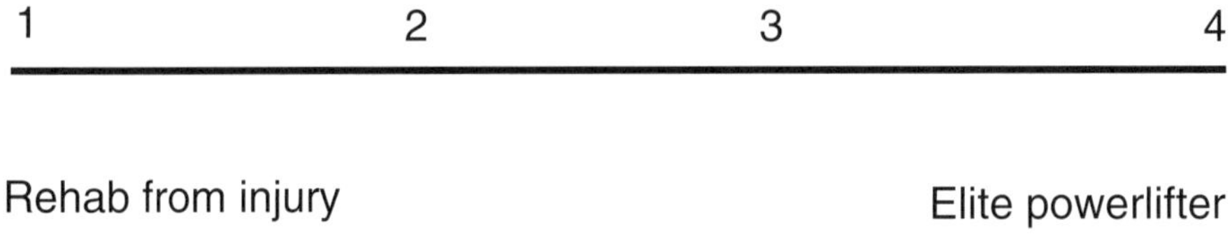

1	2	3	4

Rehab from injury   Elite powerlifter

FIGURE 3.1   Strength-level scale.

• **Limited strength.** A person with limited capacity who is either recovering from an injury or limited by orthopedic or other problems should be concerned with developing a tolerance for exercise. Typically, this person uses high reps (usually 12 to 15) with light weight to enhance the muscle education process (neurological training). Initially, this program includes single-set exercises and works the entire body. In cases where specific function is being restored, the person may perform additional sets or specific range-of-motion work to help with recovery. The goal is to establish proper technique and to slowly increase the resistance to enhance recovery and prevent injury.

• **Basic strength.** This is the base level of strength necessary to perform regular fitness tasks, play sports, and hang out in a gym. This level of strength is required for an average person to work out for general fitness. Typically, a person at this level is able to work well within his own body weight but may have trouble performing well-executed weight training exercises under a strenuous load. The goal at this level is to develop proper lifting technique and balance while performing 10 to 12 repetitions of each exercise.

- **Sport strength.** This is the level needed to make gains in power training. You can begin power training at any point, but once a solid strength base is attained, power training becomes much easier. This athlete trains with heavy weight, completing five to eight repetitions of the main exercises, which are multijoint rather than isolating one particular muscle or muscle group.

- **Powerlifter strength.** Without a doubt, powerlifters are the strongest athletes in the world, but they are not always the best athletes. Too much strength is usually not considered a hindrance, but too much strength at the expense of speed is. If you are already at the sport strength level, you are ready to begin specific training for powerlifting. However, make sure this is the level your sport requires, because powerlifters often become bulky and slow as a result of this training. Powerlifters train with very heavy weight for three to five repetitions.

Table 3.1 provides guidelines for performing strength exercises based on your strength level. Although many periodization advocates believe you should move through each phase (muscle size to peaking) in four- to eight-week blocks, my experience shows that you should concentrate only on the exercises and workouts that will improve your sports performance. If your sport does not require single-rep, explosive activity, there is no need to peak. Each phase will last as long as you need. During the season, your resistance training will decrease, and exercises should be multijoint and sport specific. The off-season allows for more variation.

Table 3.1   *Strength Training Progressions*

	Muscle size	Strength	Power	Peaking
Sets	2–4	2–5	3–5	1–3
Reps	10–12	6–8	3–5	1–3
Volume	High	High	low	Low
Intensity	Low	Medium high	High	Very high
Rest time	30–90 sec	90 sec–3 min	3–5 min	5+ min

Although strength is essential, it is only one indicator of sports success. In fact, many coaches emphasize speed training over strength training at the collegiate and professional levels. Being able to bench press 300 pounds is plenty for most sports. Going for the 400-pound barrier may not be necessary. And although it looks impressive to load weight onto the bar in the gym, it is far more impressive to break through a pack of would-be tacklers on your way to the end zone for the winning touchdown! Because each person is different, it is hard to say how much strength you need; however, if you are being beaten on the field, chances are you need more speed and power.

Current fitness   Not only is it important to know your strength levels, but assessing your general fitness level is important as well. Are you flexible? If you need blocks or plates under your heels during squats, perhaps the flexibility in your gastrocs and soleus is not up to par. Or maybe your ability to withstand extra reps and extra sets is poor, which indicates you need to work on overall conditioning. If you are not conditioned, and you are inflexible, you will have difficulty producing maximal power when doing specific exercises.

Your sport's physical requirements   When developing your base strength exercise program, refer to the power continuum and ask yourself the following questions:

1. Does your sport require efforts of long, slow duration or fast, powerful play executions?
   - Slower movements mean that true strength may be the best solution. Faster movements are power or speed dominant.
2. Does your sport require more muscle strength or more muscle endurance?
   - Typically, if you must move a lightweight implement or your own body weight, your sport requires endurance, which is best developed through a general speed-strength type of workout. If your sport requires more muscle strength, you need strength-speed workouts.
3. Do you perform one specific movement repetitively, or do the movements constantly change?
   - If the movements are fast and repetitive, it is best to work at the speed end of the continuum. If the movements are slow and repetitive, working at the strength end is better.
4. Does your sport require complex skills, or are the movements more general?
   - General movements benefit from pure-strength or strength-speed workouts. Sports consisting of complex skills benefit from speed workouts. Proper technique during the exercises is essential; therefore, it is best to start with general base strength exercises while perfecting form.

Next, you need to evaluate the potential for injury.

1. Are several joints involved in each movement?
   - Movement generated across many joints, such as serving a tennis ball, usually indicates the need for speed. Speed movements require the whole body to generate force and thus have a greater potential for injury amongst opposing muscles.
2. Does your sport include contact and collision?
   - Lots of contact indicates that power or even strength-speed is required, because the body or parts of the body must accelerate during impact,

not absorb it. For example, a boxer will continue his punch "through" his opponent, and a tackler would knock over his opponent, not stop at him. If you were to accelerate then slow down at impact, you would have no "real" effect (i.e., a boxer pushing your head rather than punching you in the head).

3. Is your sport played indoors? Outdoors? On what type of playing surface?

- Surface determines whether or not impact strategies for particular joints such as the knees and ankles are required. If there is a potential for the foot to grip the ground and become stuck, knee and ankle strengthening are essential to reduce the potential for injury.

If you answered yes to any of these questions or all three, then you need to do some "extra" work to reduce injuries. Prevention and preparation for injuries through proper training cannot be overemphasized. The more likely or the more vulnerable the body is to impact during your sport, the more you need to concentrate on strength development. Athletes in high-impact sports should spend lots of time in the base-building phase to increase tendon and ligament strength and overall joint stability.

Individualization   Finally, remember that no matter what your strength or fitness level, each athlete responds differently to training. Coaches must separate athletes and focus on individual training goals. Athletes must compare themselves, at their specific positions, to others in their sport to truly assess their weaknesses. When developing a specific strength training program, and ultimately a power program, coaches must group athletes who work well with each other, but also group together those who are at similar strength levels. Productive workouts are achieved when athletes with similar skills are matched so that friendly competition occurs during every training session. This is much more effective than pairing a 200-pound bench presser with 400-pound presser.

GENERAL GUIDELINES FOR BASE BUILDING

All training programs are composed of eight general aspects: stretching and flexibility, cardiovascular conditioning, strength training, speed and agility work, sport-specific skill training, hydration and nutrition, injury prevention, and rest, rehab, and recovery. Although this book focuses primarily on power and speed and agility work, each component is briefly described as follows.

Stretching and flexibility   Stretching is very important for your sport-specific program. The stretching program should take at least 15 minutes using a complete upper- and lower-body set of static (holding) stretches lasting 20 to 30 seconds each. Although some athletes prefer ballistic (bouncing-type) stretches, a solid static routine mixed in with an active warm-up better achieves the desired loosening and prefiring effects. Ballistic activity should be incorporated during

Sports such as baseball require players to have a combination of all the components of base building.

a well-designed pregame or prepractice warm-up that prepares muscles for their tasks. Stretching routines should address the muscles that are most vulnerable to injury, such as the hamstrings, calves, groin, and low back. Partner-assisted stretches provide a greater range of motion and are encouraged if applicable. For a comprehensive stretching guide, refer to Michael Alter's *Sport Stretch,* published by Human Kinetics in 1998, for specific stretches for your sport.

Cardiovascular conditioning   It is important to have a good aerobic base even if you participate in a sport such as golf or bowling that doesn't require much aerobic capacity. After you achieve an aerobic base, your conditioning should match your sport's aerobic and anaerobic requirements.

   To compete over a long game and, more important, a long season, you must be in supreme shape. Interval training of either short-burst, repetitive sprints for explosive athletes or longer duration intervals that alternate jogging and sprinting for endurance athletes should be integrated into the weekly overall training program. The greater the cardiovascular demand of your sport, the more time you will spend training this aspect.

   You must determine whether your sport is aerobic (composed of long-duration activity) or anaerobic (composed of short-duration activity) or a combination of both. The easiest way to determine the aerobic requirement is to separate sports into three categories: those with plays or sustained activity that lasts less than 20 seconds such as baseball; lasts more than 20 seconds but less than three minutes like hockey and basketball; or lasts more than three minutes, possibly soccer, but most likely distance track events. Further, you need to examine the rest period between each play or active period. If the rest period is less than six times the duration (less than 120 seconds of rest for every 20 seconds of activity) and the plays are repetitive, then you must train the aerobic and anaerobic systems. With rest periods exceeding 10 times the play duration, the sport is considered entirely anaerobic. This leads to the use of interval training, which may be the preferred training method because you can perform more reps at a high intensity. Refer to table 3.2 for guidelines.

Table 3.2 Endurance-Building Workout

Type of activity	Distance per rep	Time per rep	Rest
Aerobic	Long (800 m or longer)	3–15 min	3–10 min
Anaerobic and aerobic	Medium (100-800 m)	20 sec–2 min	45 sec–3 min
Anaerobic	Short (less than 100 m)	3–20 sec	20–60 sec

The number of intervals should progress gradually, and the progression will vary for each individual. Typically, an aerobic interval workout will consist of 2 to 5 long reps, a combination anaerobic and aerobic interval workout will consist of 5 to 10 reps, and an anaerobic interval workout will consist of 10 to 30 short reps. The intensity should be near maximal for each effort. In other words, you should complete the rep, but require the recovery. Carefully monitor your intensity throughout the workout. You want to put forth as much effort as you can for the workout, but you must be able to finish the last interval. The first part of the workout will feel relatively easy, and the last few repeats will take concentration and effort. Note: If you are training anaerobically (and especially for power as we will see later) then the rest is essential and it is a function of how hard you work, plus your aerobic/anaerobic goal.

Strength training   One school of thought in strength training is that weightlifting exercises should mimic the movements you perform in sports so that you can build strength while practicing specific skills. The idea is that this will cause skill transfer to occur more quickly. However, it is nearly impossible to duplicate sports movements in the weight room. Therefore, this book takes you through the steps to create maximal power and sport-specific strength through an integrated training program. The purpose of the base-building phase is not to mimic sport skills, but to allow the entire body to develop and adapt to the stresses of training and competition. The most effective skill transfer occurs when practicing skills as the body becomes stronger, faster, and more efficient. The athlete should strengthen all the muscles used to produce a movement, then practice that movement. In base building, you should emphasize the muscles that are used most frequently. A large part of developing the proper overall program is deciding on the appropriate number of sets and reps for your weight training workouts. Table 3.3 gives suggestions for a few sports.

Table 3.3 *Sport-Specific Endurance Workouts*

Sport	Number of sets	Number of reps	Intensity level	Rest (sec)
Basketball	2–4	10–15	High	30–60
Volleyball	2–5	6–10	Very high	60–150
Tennis	2–5	10–15	High	30–60
Soccer	2–3	10–20	Moderate	15–45
Golf	2–4	8–15	Moderate-high	60–150
Swimming	1–3	10–20	Moderate	15–45
Crew and rowing	3–5	8–15	Moderate-high	30–90

Speed and agility work   One of the major differences that separates athletes from weekend warriors is the extra time spent on speed and agility. Agility work, which focuses on rapid changes of direction and footwork, is necessary for almost all sports. Agility drill duration should be determined according to the sport's demands. For example, basketball, volleyball, and tennis agility drills should cover 5 to 10 yards between markers with two to five direction changes, and the athlete should keep her head up as if she were following a ball. If the footwork in your sport includes shuffle steps, backpedals, or crossover steps, incorporate these into your program. For added difficulty and variety, time the drills and perform them head to head if possible.

Leg speed is extremely important in sports such as soccer, tennis, and basketball. Speed drills should emphasize technique, and the length of each drill should be appropriate for the sport. For example, it is not necessary for a tennis player to run 40 yards because his side of the court is not that long. You can improve your speed by either increasing the strength of the leg push-off to gain a longer stride or increasing how quickly your leg cycles through the stride, or both. You can train both stride length and frequency; however, it is usually easier and less time consuming to train leg push-off strength. When training speed and agility, perform all exercises rapidly with maximal effort and power. This requires the rest time between drills to be relatively long, 60 seconds or longer, so that the rest is 6 to 10 times longer than the exercise duration. Don't confuse sprint training with conditioning. Although both might include running drills, the purpose of sprint training is to improve sprint mechanics and therefore speed. The purpose of conditioning is to improve your cardiovascular system.

Sport-specific skill training   Don't forget what has brought you to the peak of your game—technical skill. All great athletes from Michael Jordan to Tiger Woods will tell you that you must spend hours perfecting the skills of your sport. Although speed and strength will definitely help you become a better athlete, specific skill training will make you a better player. It is especially important to keep working on specific sports movements if you engage in heavy strength ing to increase your speed, strength, and mass. For example, if a tennis engages in strenuous weight training without practicing her stroke, she would have to retrain herself to compensate for the changes the increased strength causes in her swing. Therefore, even in the off-season, spend 30 minutes or so one or two days a week practicing sport-specific skills.

Hydration and nutrition   Staying properly hydrated may be the most important thing an athlete can do to improve performance. Dehydration occurs because all too often an athlete is concerned with appearance. As I tell athletes, I would rather be a better player than look good while playing. Proper hydration includes consuming 96 to 128 ounces of liquid per day. It's important to note that extreme activities can result in 3 percent or more body-weight water loss during an event (which is considered clinically dehydrated)! Remember to drink before, during, and after exercise or events, not only when you feel thirsty.

Proper nutrition is also important for peak athletic performance. Foods should contain the proper vitamins and minerals; if they don't, take multivitamins. Supplementing your diet with protein and carbohydrate shakes or drinks is not recommended unless you don't have time for regular meals, or you use them in addition to regular meals. Don't use supplements by themselves if you are trying to lose weight. It is better to eat properly. And don't be misled by the current trend of consuming large amounts of protein. Carbohydrates provide energy for training and competition in most sports. Therefore, most athletes should eat well-rounded meals high in complex carbohydrates to produce energy for extended periods. Consuming too much protein and not enough carbohydrates will severely limit your overall energy capacity, which will limit your performance. Protein should account for only 12 to 17 percent of your caloric intake (20 to 25 percent is the upper limit). More than this will cause lethargy. So before you worry about consuming enough protein, make sure you can complete your workout or, better yet, compete fiercely to the very end of your event.

Injury prevention   As noted earlier in this chapter, injury prevention is an important part of any training program, and progress must come at a steady rate if you want to avoid early retirement. You are of no value to your team or yourself sitting on the bench (unless you look good in a skirt and can yell, "D-FENCE!" loudly). Obviously, injury hinders playing performance. Therefore, you must include injury prevention tactics in your workouts. Although it is important to remember proper technique and mechanics while lifting, extra exercises and drills can strengthen areas you may not normally target. For example, you can strengthen the rotator cuff muscles to prevent shoulder problems, or target the anterior and posterior tibialis muscles and calf muscles to prevent shin splints. You can incorporate various exercises into your workout using quick circuits (circuit training, where one exercise follows another with little rest). Usually opposing muscle groups are trained that way for time constraint issues. The most important, and often overlooked, areas of an athlete's body are the abdominals and low back. A comprehensive stretching routine and core strengthening program are imperative. It is not enough to add a set of abs or hyperextensions at the end of a workout. You must concentrate on these weak areas and address them with the same seriousness with which you would approach the muscles that produce sport-specific movement.

Rest, rehab, and recovery   We've all heard the saying, "No pain, no gain." However, it is true only if pain is defined as "the extra effort and discipline required to become a champion." Building up lactic acid causes a burning sensation, which is OK. But continuing to work to the point of injury is not.

You do not have to be a sport scientist to know when you are working too hard. A breakdown in technique signals the onset of fatigue. A few more reps or seconds may be OK, but as technique continues to deteriorate, the potential for injury increases. You must stop when you need to. Remember, there is a considerable difference between *stopping* and *quitting.* Only you can determine if you're stopping because continuing would be detrimental, or taking the easy path and quitting. Knowing the difference is a step towards becoming a champion.

Another important component of a proper training program is adequate rest. Progressing carefully in your workouts prevents overtraining. Before you begin a workout, be sure you have recovered properly from the last one. Low-level, dull muscle soreness may be normal, but sharp pain indicates that you haven't completely recovered, and you may need to seek medical attention. Also, if you are overcoming an injury, be sure to follow proper rehab exercises; don't cut your rehab program short when you start feeling better. You should complete your rehab even if you have begun a solid strength training program, and preventative maintenance should always be carried out (meaning shoulder and ankle pre-hab programs). A sound rehab program will return you to training quickly, but more important, it will prevent recurring and chronic injury.

In addition to the eight components of base building, you should also keep in mind the KISS (keep it simple, stupid) principle when designing a training program. Do not try to learn so many drills and exercises that you can't do any of them properly. A common temptation is to incorporate new exercises into your program because you've heard they are good, or because some famous athlete does them. Every time you introduce something new, you must take time to learn proper technique and execution. You may not always have enough time. Even a beneficial exercise may not be a good choice for you if it takes too long to master. Instead, learn a few drills and exercises so that you can perform them with good technique. Quality always wins over quantity (except maybe in the case of your bank balance). Also, it's important to remember that, when designing your training program, the goal is to become better at your specific sport, not at each specific exercise that you choose (although that will occur). Therefore, three other key points should be noted.

• **Concentration exercises are out.** Concentration, or isolation, exercises should not be nixed forever, but added at the end of the workout once the main work has been done. Although bodybuilding routines increase size, your main objective is to improve sports performance. Multijoint movements or compound exercises with variations in movements will increase your body's kinesthetic awareness (a fancy term for balance and coordination), while increasing strength. Because time is always an issue, keep your isolation exercises in small amounts and last on your list. Add these to your workout through supersets or circuit-type exercises in between your main lifts. For example, after a set of squats, hit your abs while giving your legs a break.

• **Pace is essential.** Keep a workout pace that is fast and furious. Long rest periods will not prepare you to handle the rigors of sport. Remember, volume must be moderate to high; therefore, getting everything done requires a quick pace. Take no more than 90 seconds between sets, including the superset exercises.

• **Recovery is necessary.** The term *recovery* describes the process by which energy systems regain their fuel supply and remove metabolic waste. After vigorous exercise, the entire body must recover; however, during repetitive exercise or back-to-back activity such as tournament games, complete recovery may not be possible. Fatigue occurs for a variety of reasons and is discussed in detail in later chapters. One of the major sources of fatigue is high levels of lactic acid in the muscles. The intensity and duration of the anaerobic exercise determines how much lactic acid accumulates. Lactic acid is a byproduct of anaerobic glycolysis (the breakdown by the body of carbohydrates as glucose by way of phosphate derivatives). To be able to perform at your best and stay healthy, it's important to remove lactic acid or recover from its effects between bouts of exercise. Depending on how much lactic acid has accumulated, it can take an hour or more to completely clear if the recovery process consists of rest. Light aerobic exercise, or active recovery, clears lactic acid in about half that time. And half the accumulated lactic acid may clear in as few as five minutes. Long-duration aerobic activity also requires a recovery process. If true fatigue occurs because of glycogen depletion, such as the fatigue seen in a marathoner unable to complete a race, complete recovery may take a few days to two weeks. The recovery process after aerobic activity typically takes one to four hours. In general, the restoration of glycogen, phosphagens, and body temperature during recovery are dictated by the duration and intensity of the exercise, as well as dietary intake before and after exercise.

YOUR INDIVIDUALIZED PROGRAM

With your toolbox containing the eight components of a training prescription in place, you are ready to set the foundation for your training program. The first few workouts or weeks are called the tissue adaptation phase. A general tissue adaptation cycle consists of exercises using a moderate weight, enough to challenge but not exhaust, and about 10 reps per set. You should start with a single set, and by the end of the adaptation period, be able to perform two or three sets with a challenging weight. During this base-building period, perform general exercises that work all parts of the body. Perform resistance training four times a week. A complete-body routine three times a week also works, but because the emphasis is base building, concentrating on specific areas sets the foundation more securely. Table 3.4 outlines a routine that groups upper-body and lower-body exercises, split over four days.

Table 3.4 Four-Day Rotational Strength Workout

Days 1 and 3: Upper body	Days 2 and 4: Lower body
Bench press	Squat or leg press
Seated row	Leg extension
Incline press or military press	Hamstring curl
Lat pull-down	Lunge
Lateral raise	Heel raise
Shrug	Toe pull (for anterior tibialis)
Triceps extension	Abdominal
Biceps curl	Low back extension
Rotator cuff circuit	Ankle circuit

To continue with our house-building analogy, a house's exterior walls support the roof. And within the house are walls that separate space into rooms. When building a training program, the basic program, or exterior walls, supports the training goal, in your case, increasing power. And each training modality, or interior wall, specifically addresses a training need (much like each room in a house serves a particular purpose). Once you have determined your goal and built a base, the program design will focus on helping you reach the goal. To increase power you must achieve the optimal combination of speed and strength; therefore, every component of your training should move you closer to that goal.

Specifically, your power training program will combine speed and strength to provide power (the roof of your house). And just as the roof of a house protects the interior and prevents the harsh environment from entering, power will enhance the athlete. A powerful athlete not only prevails in competition, but is also prepared for the explosive nature of some sports, which decreases the chance for injury.

Looking back over our house, we see that our base-building program usually consists of sets of 10 reps and as we refine the walls and roof, we move toward lower reps executed much more rapidly. The house analogy serves to bring us from a general solid foundation to our peak.

Jostling for position in lacrosse is a powerful movement that is a combination of speed and strength.

As a responsible homeowner, you need to maintain your house and perform upgrades as sections begin to deteriorate. So too do you need to assess your program. This is the only way to make sure that your program is working effectively and helping you reach your goal. More important, this is where you have a chance to reevaluate and replan your goals, or develop a more specific program. Feedback is the key. Your feedback is self-monitored; you decide whether the program is working based on the notes you keep on your progress. If you are not making gains, look back over your results to try to figure out why. For example, you may have been injured or took time off, both counterproductive to reaching goals. If you have been working hard, but results are beginning to slow, chapter 9, the chapter on periodization, can help you figure out how to solve this problem.

General Base-Building Exercises

Basic strength is best built through multijoint exercises with movement patterns similar to those in your sport. Although no exercise can duplicate sports movement, the intent of base training is to develop proper technique and movement patterns and to strengthen the entire joint capsule and surrounding musculature. The following exercises provide a foundation. Because proper technique is key, be sure you can perform the lifts properly; otherwise choose exercises that require less skill, for example, use machines instead of free weights. We start with some information and exercises on key stability areas (ankles and shoulders) to prevent injury and then follow with general base-building mini programs and exercises. Be sure to choose exercises depending on your sport's needs based on its location on the speed–strength continuum.

Stability and Strength Exercises

Oddly enough, one of the least trained areas of the body is responsible for absorbing 99 percent of all the force transmitted through the body, so it's important that we ensure stability in this area before moving on to our core exercises. And what's more, this same area, the ankle and foot, initiates almost all sporting movements through its interaction with the ground. It is puzzling that coaches seem to forget how important the ankle is.

The ankle is the foundation for force development, with strong support on the medial (inside) side of the ankle but rather weak support on the lateral (outside) side. Rolling the ankle occurs when you land on the outside of the foot and the ankle rolls inward. This is a common injury in basketball, volleyball, and other jumping sports. A decade or two ago, it was common for athletes to "walk on their ankles" (walk on the outsides of the feet with the bottom of the feet turned in) as part of their warm-up exercises. I recall wondering the purpose of the drill when I played football; it is much clearer now.

Like the ankle, the shoulder capsule is often neglected in training. Considering the velocity of shoulder rotation during throwing and punching, this area must be targeted during base building. Because the deltoid muscle is heavily worked all week during training and practice, it fatigues relatively quickly. Unfortunately, the traditional military presses or front and lateral raises do not help the capsule strengthen on their own. Therefore, it is necessary to isolate the rotator cuff muscles and perform a separate shoulder training circuit. Unlike the ankle, though, the movement at the shoulder is performed at much higher speeds but with much less overall loading. Rather than increasing rotator cuff strength (not that it isn't important but it will strengthen anyway), you want to increase the velocity of movement during base building.

Shoulder exercises should target all of the muscles that surround the capsule. Therefore, you must train the muscles responsible for moving the joint through each plane of movement. The major rotator cuff movements are internal and external rotation and must be performed in multiple planes.

Incorporating the ankle and shoulder training into the regular base-building program is not always easy. Often athletes are tired from training and find the additional exercises boring and fatiguing. The ankles can be trained right before lower-body strengthening work or right after, because typical weight training does not emphasize the ankle musculature. If the athlete's training includes running- and jumping-type movements, ankle strengthening should follow the workout. Rotator cuff training should almost always follow upper-body training. If the rotator cuff muscles become too fatigued before major upper-body lifting, they will be unable to support the heavier training. Both the ankle and shoulder training programs should be done twice a week for at least four weeks and preferably eight or even regularly throughout the year.

Ankle Exercises

Four-way ankle exercises that tax all the muscles surrounding the ankle and foot will improve the overall strength of the ankles. They are also more effective than exercises that focus on just one aspect, such as calf exercises. A strong ankle capsule will not prevent the ankle from rolling, but it will prevent injuries when it does roll. The strategy for a strong ankle is to work the weakest side through to the strongest. Because calf exercises are a basic part of most athletes' training, I try to concentrate on three major exercises. Begin with eversion (*a*), then inversion (*b*), and finally work on dorsiflexion (*c*). Start by using relatively light resistance and working 12 to 15 reps. Finish a four-week ankle program with eight-rep sets with maximal weight. Table 3.5 outlines a four-week program. Because it

a

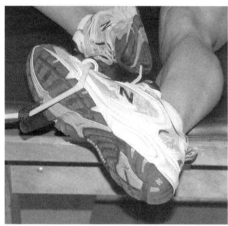

b

c

Table 3.5 Four-Week Ankle Stability Training Schedule

Exercise	Week 1	Week 2	Week 3	Week 4
Eversion	3 × 15	3 × 12	3 × 10	3 × 8
Inversion	3 × 15	3 × 12	3 × 10	3 × 8
Dorsiflexion	3 × 15	3 × 12	3 × 10	3 × 8

is difficult to find machines for these exercises, they can be done with resistive tubing as shown in the photos or against manual resistance. Ankle work can be done when calf work would normally be done on a leg day.

Shoulder Exercises

To achieve a well-conditioned shoulder capsule, you must perform internal and external rotation in four positions. In position 1 (*a*), the arm is flexed and tight to the body. In position 2 (*b*), the arm is abducted (parallel to the ground) 90 degrees at the shoulder and the elbow is flexed at 90 degrees (like making a "stop" signal). In position 3 (*c*), the arm is abducted at 90 degrees, with the arm extended at the elbow (straight out to the side parallel to the ground). In position 4 (*d*), the arm is fully extended straight overhead. With the arms fully extended, the rotation is small; therefore, the larger pectoralis, latissimus dorsi, and deltoid muscles do much of the work. Move the muscles through the greatest range of motion possible. In this type of training, start with controlled, slow-moving sets of eight reps, one set per position both internally (I) and externally (E). Slowly increase velocity and reps over a four-week period. Table 3.6 outlines a four-week program.

a

b

c

d

Table 3.6   *Four-Week Shoulder Stability Training Schedule*

Exercise	Week 1	Week 2	Week 3	Week 4
Position 1 - I	1 × 8	1 × 8	1 × 10	1 × 12
Position 1 - E	1 × 8	1 × 8	1 × 10	1 × 12
Position 2 - I	1 × 8	1 × 8	1 × 10	1 × 12
Position 2 - E	1 × 8	1 × 8	1 × 10	1 × 12
Position 3 - I	1 × 8	1 × 8	1 × 10	1 × 12
Position 3 - E	1 × 8	1 × 8	1 × 10	1 × 12
Position 4 - I	1 × 8	1 × 8	1 × 10	1 × 12
Position 4 - E	1 × 8	1 × 8	1 × 10	1 × 12

I = internal and E = external

Squat

Start by positioning the bar across the shoulders with the load distributed across the mass of the back. Make sure the hands are positioned as close to the center of the bar as possible; the head is up, and the chest is out; the shoulders are back, and the back is flat with a slight arch at the base. The feet are shoulder-width apart.

To begin the descent phase, back slowly out of the racks. Keep the feet shoulder-width apart and point the toes slightly outward at an angle of 30 to 35 degrees. Inhale deeply and contract the muscles of the torso to help stabilize the upper body. Keep the feet flat on the ground and descend slowly by lowering the buttocks toward the floor. Descend until the tops of the thighs are slightly lower than parallel with the floor. Keep the hips under the bar as much as possible to prevent the torso from leaning too far forward (*a*).

The ascent starts with a powerful drive to accelerate the weight out of the bottom position. Keep the head up to help counter a forward lean. Once the bar has started moving upward, thrust the hips forward to place them under the bar. When the bar has passed through the sticking point, start to exhale through the mouth. Keep the muscles of the torso contracted throughout the ascent phase of the lift. Come to full knee lockout, and replace the bar in the rack (*b*).

a

b

Lunge

Begin by standing upright with the bar across the back (as in a squat) or weights in the hands. For proper back alignment, keep the head up and the chest out. Step forward about three feet.

On the descent, the front leg should bend similarly to the squat in that the knee should not lower over the toe. Step forward (*a*), bending at the knee so that the upper leg is about parallel to the floor. The trail leg should bend until the knee is about two inches from the floor (*b*).

The front-leg ascent is similar to the squat and the trail leg extends; however, when performing walking lunges, the trail leg can be dragged up for balance before moving to the next rep. Make sure to maintain proper back alignment throughout the exercise.

a　　　　　　　　　　　　　　　　　*b*

Leg Extension

Start by sitting upright on the leg extension machine. The knees should be bent at a 90-degree angle and the leg pad should lie across the shin just above the ankle. Line up the knees with the machine's axis of rotation (*a*).

To perform the exercise, straighten the knees until the lower legs are parallel to the floor (*b*). Return the weight to the starting position in a controlled manner.

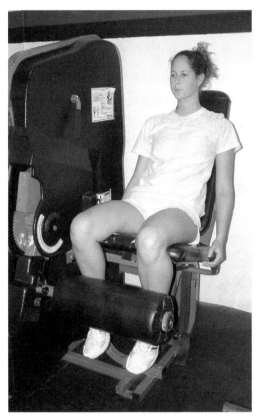

a

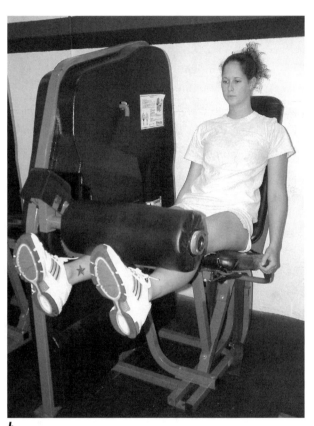

b

Hamstring Curl

Start by lying face down on the leg curl machine. Position the knees just off the end of the bench. Place the heels under the heel pads and hold onto the bench or handles (*a*).

Keeping the upper body flat against the bench, raise the heel pads toward the buttocks (*b*). When the full range of movement has been completed, lower the weight to the starting position.

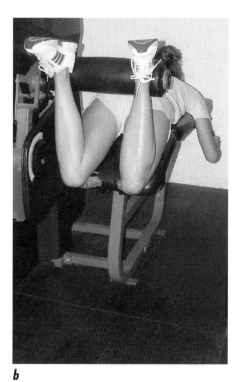

a   *b*

Arm Curl

Start by taking an underhand grip (for sport athletes usually free-weight barbells or dumbbells are used). The hands are shoulder-width apart and the arms are straight. The knees are slightly bent. The torso is upright and doesn't sway.

To perform the exercise, bend the elbows so that the weight finishes just under the chin. Maintaining control, lower the weight until the arms are straight.

Side Lateral Raise

Start by holding a dumbbell in each hand just in front of the thighs with the palms facing each other. The body is upright and the elbows are bent slightly.

To perform the exercise, keep the elbows slightly bent and raise the weight to the side until the arms reach shoulder level and are parallel to the floor. Lower the weight to the start position.

Dumbbell Arm Curl

Start by holding a dumbbell in each hand, hands hanging down on each side of the body, with the palms facing the legs. The arms are straight and the knees slightly bent. The torso is upright and doesn't sway.

To perform the exercise, bend the elbow and rotate the palms (*a*) so that the weight finishes at the shoulder (*b*). Lower the weight under control until the arms are straight.

a *b*

Seated Overhead Press

Start by sitting on a bench or military press machine with the bar in back of the head and the hands slightly wider than shoulder-width apart. Keep the torso upright and contracted. The feet should be flat on the floor (a).

Keeping the muscles of the torso contracted, push the weight overhead until the arms lock out (b). Lower the weight until the bar touches the top of the trapezius. Prevent the body from leaning backward by keeping the abdominal muscles tightly contracted.

a

b

Seated Overhead Dumbbell Press

Start by sitting on a bench, grasping a dumbbell in each hand. Bring the dumb-bells to the shoulders, palms facing forward. The hands are slightly wider than shoulder-width apart and the feet are flat on the floor. Keep the torso upright and contracted (*a*).

Keeping the muscles of the torso contracted, push the weight overhead until the arms lock out (*b*). Lower the dumbbell to the top of the trapezius. Prevent the body from leaning backward by contracting the abdominal muscles.

a

b

Barbell Shrug

Start by standing upright. Using an overhand grip with the hands about shoulder-width apart, hold the bar in front of the thighs close to the body.

To perform the exercise, raise the shoulders toward the ears, then lower them slowly to the starting position.

Preacher Curl

Start by holding a barbell or the handles of a preacher curl machine with the hands about shoulder-width apart in an underhand grip with the arms straight. Bend the knees slightly. Place the upper arm over the preacher bench so that the chest rests across the back of the bench. The torso is upright and doesn't sway (*a*).

To perform the exercise, bend the elbows so that the weight finishes just under the chin (*b*). Lower the weight under control until the arms are straight.

a

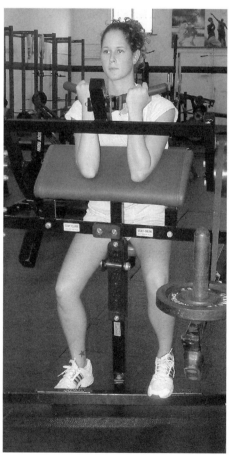

b

Lat Pull-Down

Start in a seated position. Extend the arms overhead, and grasp the bar with a wide palms-down grip (*a*).

To perform the exercise, pull the bar down in front of the body until it touches the top of the sternum (*b*). The bar may also be pulled behind the head until it touches the base of the neck. Extend the arms to return the bar to the starting position.

a

b

Lying Barbell Triceps Extension (Skull Crusher)

Start by lying flat on a bench with the feet flat on the floor. Grasp the barbell with an overhand grip, with the hands six to eight inches apart and the arms extended over the chest (*a*).

Bend the elbows to lower the weight until the bar touches behind the forehead. The elbows should point toward the ceiling (*b*). Return the weight to the starting position.

a

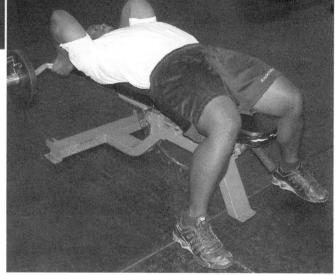

b

Triceps Push-Down

Start by standing in front of a lat pull-down machine or cable tower. With the body upright, grasp the bar in an overhand grip with the hands six to eight inches apart. The elbows are at the sides, and the hands are level with the shoulders (a).

To perform the exercise, push the weight down until the arms are straight (b). Return the weight to the starting position.

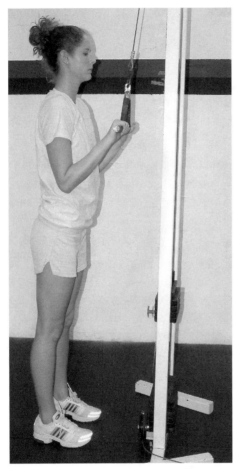
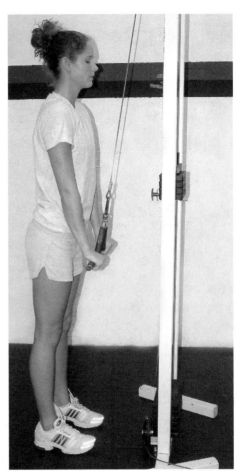

a *b*

Lying Dumbbell Triceps Extension

Start by lying face up on a bench with the feet flat on the floor. Hold a dumbbell in each hand in an overhand grip. Extend the arms over the chest (a).

To perform the exercise, bend the elbows to lower the weight until the hands are at the shoulders. The elbows should point toward the ceiling (b). Return the weight to the starting position.

a

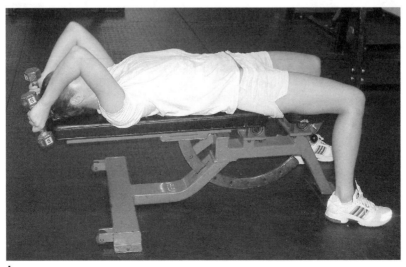

b

Seated Cable Row

Start in a seated position in a cable row machine. With the knees slightly bent, bend at the waist and grasp the handles. Pushing through the legs, pull the handles to the body and sit up straight.

To perform the exercise, keep the back straight and allow the weight to straighten the arms (*a*), then pull the handles until the hands touch the ribs (*b*).

a *b*

Bent Lateral Raise

Start by sitting on a bench and bend at the waist so that the chest rests on the thighs, keeping the upper body straight. Hold a dumbbell in each hand just behind the calves with the palms facing each other (*a*).

Keeping the elbows bent slightly, raise the weight to the side until the arms reach shoulder level and are parallel to the floor. Pause at the top of the movement (*b*). Finish the movement by lowering the arms to the start position.

a

b

Ab Curl-Up

Start by lying flat on the floor with the knees bent to about 140 degrees. Keep the feet flat on the floor and the hands on the thighs.

To perform the exercise, curl the trunk and slide the hands along the thighs until the hands reach the knees. Initiate the curl by tightening the abdominal muscles, then raising the shoulders off the ground and trying to press the back into the floor during the exercise. Slowly lower to the start position.

Base building is an essential part of the training program, however, it is not a necessary step for the "all ready" exercising athlete. For those coming back from a long off-season or summer holidays, it will certainly help get you on track. The preventative maintenance programs, however, should be a mainstay for all active athletes. A solid base builds the foundation for grueling demands of the serious athlete's strength training program.

4

Maximizing Strength

Few things are more impressive than watching a human being lift 1,000 pounds. The rate at which new strength bests are attained is almost scary. It seems like only a few years ago when the first 1,000-pound squat and 700-pound bench press were recorded. More than 1,100 pounds and 900 pounds are the records in those lifts. In fact, it took nearly 20 years to improve the bench press from the mid-600 pounds to mid-750 pounds; but it took less than two years to see the improvement from 800 to 900 pounds. How are athletes able to reach such extreme levels of strength?

As we have learned, it takes both speed and strength in the right combinations to excel at any sport. In this chapter we turn our attention to strength. Strength is a key aspect in many hitting or striking sports, because the stronger you are, the easier it is to lift or move light weights. (And if you combine that strength with speed, you will be able to move light weights quickly.) As you get stronger, you will need less energy to move light objects, such as a bat, volleyball, or tennis racket, leaving you with more energy to run across the court, jump for a rebound, or run to first base. Recall from the force–velocity curve that power is best produced at higher velocities. So naturally, when the weight is lighter, power will increase as higher velocity is achieved. Training to gain strength should be a priority in all sports, but especially in those where moving heavy objects (such as other people) is a big part of the game. To build this type of strength, a program of specific exercises is more effective than a typical bodybuilding routine, where the focus is on building size rather than strength. You must develop strength that you can use during your sport. This is usually accomplished through multijoint exercises. Strength training also targets the largest muscle groups, because the larger muscles are capable of producing greater strength. However, it is fruitless to train muscles to be stronger if those particular strong muscles are not needed in your sport. And finally, strength training is not like most fashionable gym workouts that focus on individual body parts rather than training to sculpt a body characterized by symmetry, big arms, and a ripped abdominal region. You will focus on increasing the weight you can bench press, squat, and row in order to build useable strength rather than bulk. Although strength training will increase muscle size, the focus is on movement technique and exercise execution.

In the previous chapter, we saw that you must lay a training base before working toward further gains in any aspect of training. And strength training is probably the most similar in methodology to building the base. Since strength training deals mostly with set lifting patterns, it continues to enhance muscle size and strength. However, in strength training, unlike hypertrophy training (that which bodybuilders do), strength is developed by improving neurological functioning in addition to increasing muscle size. To lift an object of great mass, you need both timing and coordination of various muscle groups, as well as the optimal number of muscle fibers to perform the task. The term recruitment is used to describe the ability to call the maximal number of muscle fibers into action. As the weight increases, more muscle fibers are needed. By forcing the body to recruit more fibers, strength improves, and so goes the training of increasing strength through lifting heavy weights. However, being stronger does not automatically make you more powerful. To understand how strength training enhances power, let's take a look at human physiology.

A CLOSER LOOK AT MUSCLE ARCHITECTURE

The basic structure of a muscle is not too exciting. Strands of proteins (resembling a beaded necklace) are coiled with other protein strands (helical, or spiral, in nature) that interact with larger protein helical-bound strands. When these protein strands latch on to one another, they pull their respective sides together. Because the protein strands are anchored, when they pull together, muscles contract. Sarcomeres, parallel groups of anchored protein strands, are connected to one another in a series, and others are connected on top of one another in a parallel fashion (figure 4.1). Each of the thicker proteins, myosin, is surrounded by six smaller proteins, actin. When a stimulus tells the fiber to contract, heads from the myosin band reach out, grab onto the actin, and pull through. The number of heads that make contact and the speed at which they connect dictates how much force the single sarcomere produces. Because the sarcomere is microscopic, thousands of them work in unison to produce movement.

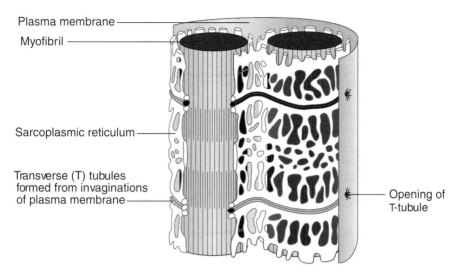

Plasma membrane

Myofibril

Sarcoplasmic reticulum

Transverse (T) tubules
formed from invaginations
of plasma membrane

Opening of
T-tubule

FIGURE 4.1   Myofibril wrapped in the sarcoplasmic reticulum.

Sarcomeres are bound together by a myofibril. Several myofibrils are bound together by the muscle fiber itself (see figure 4.2). Surrounding the muscle fiber is a membrane called the sarcoplasmic reticulum (SR). The SR transmits the action potential signal from the brain telling the muscles to contract to the muscle fiber to start the process of actin–myosin binding. In addition, the SR stores and releases calcium, which is needed for actin–myosin binding. Once the action potential reaches the membrane, it releases calcium into the muscle cell, and the contraction process begins. The more action potentials that are sent and the faster they are sent, the stronger the muscle contraction.

The transmission of force through the sarcomeres and ultimately through the entire muscle is accomplished through various protein structures that anchor the myofibrils to muscle fibers and to the entire muscle. These structures are collectively termed the series and parallel proteins of muscle. They are elastic in nature and are responsible for the elastic-like capabilities of muscle. Recall from chapter 2 where we tested for countermovement jumps. You were able to jump higher when you were able to do a countermovement (dipping down) prior to jumping. Part of the reason is that once you stretch a muscle (eccentric action of the quadriceps and glutes when you dip down), you gain increased force from its ability to recoil back (like a stretched

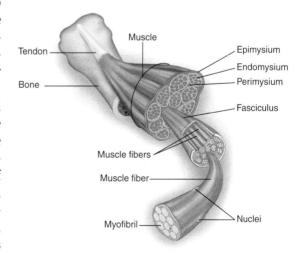

Muscle

Tendon

Bone

Epimysium

Endomysium

Perimysium

Fasciculus

Muscle fibers

Muscle fiber

Myofibril

Nuclei

FIGURE 4.2   Structure of the muscle.

rubber band) in addition to its regular force-generating capacities. You will see this concept in action in chapter 7 on plyometrics.

BASIC MUSCLE MECHANICS

Three biomechanical characteristics affect muscle strength. The first is the size or shape of the muscle and its ability to recruit muscle fibers. There are six primary types of muscle shapes (not discussed in this text), each with various numbers and types of muscle fibers. The length of the muscle also affects strength. A short muscle can generate force rapidly by increasing the length of the lever moment arm. Also, the shorter the myofibril, the quicker it can contract completely. The muscle's origin and where it attaches also affect muscle strength. Where the muscle fiber attaches affects the length of the lever moment arm.

Therefore, short people are well suited for weight training; it's a leverage thing. Two bones, a joint, and a muscle form a relatively simple lever system. The muscles that span a joint contract to move the bones. The joint acts as a fulcrum for which the lever system is created. The complex part of movement is getting the levers to work together.

Muscle Fiber Types

There are three basic types of muscle fibers in the human body. They are named according to their function: slow twitch (ST), fast glycolitic (FG) or fast twitch (FT IIb), and fast oxidative glycolitic (FOG or FT IIa). Fiber type is primarily determined by the way in which it is innervated. In other words, the type of nerve ending at the muscle has an influential effect on the functional capabilities of the fiber.

ST muscle fibers function primarily for endurance. They contract at relatively low speeds and are primarily used during typical low- to moderate-threshold endurance-type activities. These muscle fibers have the ability to use fat, glucose (glycogen), lactic acid, and protein (to an extent) as their fuel sources. These fibers have a large number of mitochondria (fuel-processing plant) giving rise to their endurance nature. Slow-twitch fibers are recruited first, are relatively fatigue resistant, and have a relatively low force output per cross-sectional area as compared to the faster-twitch fibers.

FOG fibers are also endurance fibers. However, their main differences are in their contractile rate and force production. Consider these fibers as the "middle" fiber in that they share characteristics of both ST and FT fibers. FOG fibers contract at a rate of two to four times faster than ST fibers. FOG fibers come into play for more rapid repeated movements as may be found at higher intensity, submaximal exercise. Generally, these fibers are larger in cross-sectional area than ST fibers. These fibers have oxidative capabilities as they also have mitochondria present. When FOG fibers are the primary source of force production, lactic acid production occurs. Typically, FOG fibers are activated as anaerobic glycolysis becomes the major source of fuel production.

FG fibers are the ones responsible for high-speed force and power output. These contract at the same or slightly faster speed as FOG fibers, but they don't have the same endurance capacities. These fibers become involved in very intense anaerobic activity and are the primary type used in various forms of explosive activity. The primary source of fuel for these fibers is the rapid stores of creatine phosphate and ATP in the muscles themselves. FG fibers are highly fatigable and are usually recruited last. These fibers are larger in diameter than the FOG or ST fibers. What makes these fibers so unique is that they reach peak force output about twice as fast as their slower counterparts, but also reach a higher force output level. It is thought that an athlete possessing large numbers of these fibers distinguishes the sprinter, strength, and/or power athlete from the rest.

Much discussion has been made about whether a specific fiber can be changed from one type to another. Newer research suggests that specific training may have an impact on the adaptation of fibers while traditionalists feel much research is still needed. It would be nice to think that we can change fibers to suit our needs simply through training, however, even the research that suggests fibers may be altered has shown that it takes tremendous stimulus and may take several years for the transformations to occur. For the purposes of this book, and your training, it is not necessary to worry about fiber types, more that training in general, and specifically for power, causes the body to adapt.

A motor unit, on the other hand, is the nerve, its branches, and all the fibers that it (the nerve) innervates (see figure 4.3). A motor unit has a unique feature called the All-or-None Principle. This principle states that all the muscle fibers within a motor unit will fire when called upon. Further, the entire muscle fiber will contract completely and maximally when stimulated. It is either all, or the motor unit is not activated. The uniqueness is in the fact that each motor unit has a specific number of fibers that it stimulates (varies considerably in number) and that each muscle can have several thousand motor units within it. However, only a certain number of units may be recruited to produce a force. This is how we can distinguish exerting the amount of force necessary to lift a pencil versus lifting a 50-pound dumbbell. Therefore, while the whole muscle appears to be contracting (like in a biceps curl), depending on the resistance as compared to the athlete's maximum strength, only a certain number of motor units may actually be doing the work.

The term "selective fiber recruitment" refers to an athlete's ability to call upon the specific fiber type necessary to do the desired work. While

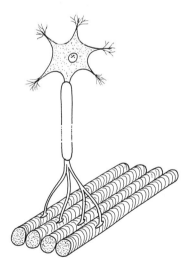

FIGURE 4.3 *A motor unit.*

we can't actually select which fibers we want to use, it appears that recruitment and selection does have a specific process. It is believed that recruitment can be trained, and hence, the power/strength athlete has the ability to recruit fast-twitch fibers better than a general athlete doing weight training. In general, as any person becomes stronger, greater recruitment is necessary. Specific types of training can aid in fiber recruitment; however, it should be noted that only an experienced lifter with a specific type of routine can enhance fiber recruitment at the advanced level. It is also important to note that although fiber recruitment occurs at all levels of muscle force production, only the very maximal force-generating potential of an entire muscle can be addressed through maximal fiber recruitment.

Each motor unit, when excited, causes the muscle fibers within the unit to contract. A single motor unit contraction is called a twitch. When multiple units twitch, the sum result gives a more forceful contraction. If a motor unit fires, then relaxes, the single twitch stands alone, but not enough force is produced long enough to move weight. If multiple twitches fire in succession, leaving little or no time for relaxation, a peak force output is reached. If peak force output is maintained by continuous multiple motor units firing, the resulting contraction or tension built up is called tetanus, or more simply, maximal output (of only the motor units called to do the task and not necessarily the entire muscle). Peak tetanus occurs within .05 seconds for FT fibers and .10 seconds for ST fibers. Peak tetanus is maintained until either the task is stopped or fatigue sets in. As fatigue of those fibers begins, more motor units may be called to action, and hence the cycle continues (see table 4.1).

Table 4.1 Characteristics of Slow- and Fast-Twitch Motor Units

	Slow twitch, fatigue resistant (S)	Fast twitch, fatigue resistant (FR)	Fast twitch, fatigable (FF)
Activation threshold of muscle fibers	Low	Moderate	High
Contraction time of fibers (ms)	100–120	40–45	40–45
Innervation ratio of motor unit	Low	Moderate	High
Type of muscle fibers	I	IIa	IIb
Type of axon	Aβ	Aα	Aα
Diameter of axon (μm)	7–14	12–20	12–20
Speed (m/sec)	40–80	65–120	65–120
Duration and size of force	Prolonged low force	Prolonged relatively high force	Intermittent high force
Type of activities	Long distance running and swimming	Kayaking and rowing	Sprinting, throwing, jumping, and weightlifting

Three Types of Levers

The three types of levers are first, second, and third class. Each class of lever offers specific mechanical advantages and disadvantages. The length of the bone and where the muscle attaches to it change the lever system's mechanical advantage (see table 4.2). To simplify the lever issue, imagine trying to open the top of a bottle with an opener that is one inch long. You have nothing to hold on to and opening it would be quite difficult. Now take a longer bottle opener; since the arm where you apply the force is longer, the top pops off easier. Or imagine trying to "ring the bell" at the fair with a sledge hammer that was only 12 inches long—winning the prize would not be possible. Using the longer sledge hammer allows for greater force to be developed—actually it is greater speed at which the hammer hits. Most of the muscle–bone systems within the body are made up of third-class levers, which are well suited to producing speed. Examples of levers capable of quick movements are muscles that extend the elbow (triceps in punching) and knee (quadriceps in kicking). Although the human body is built for speed, certain lever systems are capable of creating great force. Because the resistance in third-class levers is much farther from the fulcrum, the end of the resistance lever has to travel faster than the part near the fulcrum to reach the same point along the movement path. To understand this concept, the butt end of the baseball bat reaches the same horizontal as the end of the bat when it makes contact with the ball. Thus the longer the lever arm, the greater speed can be developed. Of course this only works provided that the implement (or body segment) is still manageable. If your bat was six feet long, it would be quite hard to handle!

Second-class levers are well designed for producing force. In actual fact, the muscles themselves do not form the lever. It is the combination of multiple joints and body position that allow for such great leverage. The most common second-class lever is made by the toe (fulcrum) and heel (where the force is applied) joints, where the gastrocnemius and soleus (calf muscles) work. That is why you sometimes see 500 pounds of weight stacked on the heel-raise machine. The mechanical advantage of second-class levers creates great force.

Not only does the type of lever matter, but also the length of the moment arm and the force generated by the muscle. The longer the moment arm, the smaller

Table 4.2 Lever Descriptions and Examples

	Fulcrum	Muscle insertion	Resistance	Example	Muscle example
First class	Middle	One end	Other end	Teeter-totter	Triceps
Second class	Other end	One end	Middle	Wheelbarrow	Gastrocnemius
Third class	One end	Middle	Other end	Baseball bat	Biceps

the amount of force required from the muscle to move the object. In figure 4.3 the muscle is at length A from the axis of rotation (the fulcrum or joint). If the muscle attached farther from the axis, the lever system would have a greater moment arm and produce greater force. In most third-class levers the muscle attaches very close to the axis of rotation (for example, the biceps), which reduces the moment arm and the force output.

Figure 4.4 illustrates a third-class lever. If the moment arm, denoted by A, were increased by moving the muscle's attachment to C, the moment arm would be equal to A + B. For example, picture the biceps in an arm curl. The biceps attach to the lower arm very close to the elbow joint. As the biceps contract and move the lower arm, the lower arm moves through a range of nearly 180 degrees. If the muscle attached near the wrist instead, moving the arm would be much easier (but we'd look funny). As the movement of the biceps curl progresses, the force required is greatest when the elbow is at a 90-degree angle because of the change in the moment arm's perpendicular distance from the line of action, as illustrated in figure 4.5.

Although the arm doesn't change length, perpendicular distance between the weight in the hand (the resistance) and the humerus or the biceps against the humerus changes throughout the movement. The line of action is the force line generated by the biceps muscle pulling upward. The curling movement changes the force required to overcome the resistance during the movement. So not only do strength factors such as limb length and muscle attachment change the force requirement, but so does the movement itself. This illustrates the complex nature of strength gain, force output, and power production. People with short limbs require less overall force to move an object, and the force must only be produced over a short distance. Tall people, on the other hand, must apply the force longer to move an object because the object must travel farther. During a bench press exercise, compare the average push distance of a person 5 feet, 6 inches tall to that of a person 6 feet, 6 inches tall. The push distance can be nearly twice as far for the taller athlete. We don't need science to figure out who must do more work. However, longer levers are not necessarily a liability. They

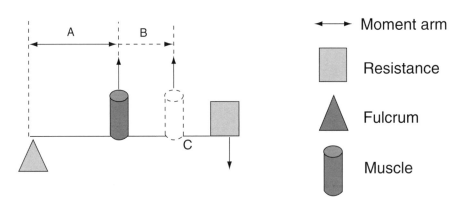

FIGURE 4.4   Third-class lever.

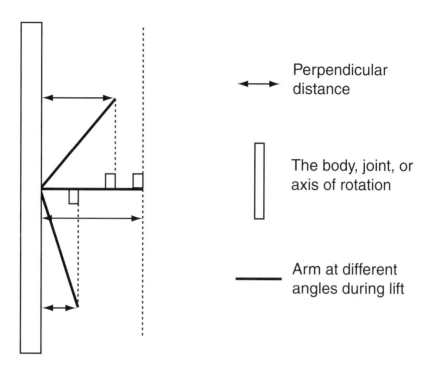

FIGURE 4.5 *Illustration of the third-class lever system at work in a biceps curl.*

can create great speed. Consider golfers and baseball players. The taller golfer or baseball player can often hit the ball farther by generating greater power if he can swing the club or bat quickly through its longer path. Of course, being taller does not necessarily make someone a better golfer or hitter; practice and skill are still essential.

Muscle Pennation

The simple lever system model helps explain how to produce force. However, the lever alone is only part of the equation, because more than one muscle acts on a joint, and most movements involve several joints working simultaneously. To further complicate matters, not all muscles are shaped the same, and thus, a muscle's line of pull is not always like that in our biceps example. Pennation describes the way muscle fibers align themselves throughout the muscle. In the common biceps (a longitudinal pennation) the line of pull is directly in line with the length of the muscle, however, several muscles in the body, such as the pectoralis, have fibers running oblique to one another allowing the muscle to perform more than one pulling action. The relative pennation of the muscle affects how a muscle produces force, and ultimately, how the muscle develops during resistance training. Therefore, you must use several methods for developing strength in order to target all of the muscles in a particular movement.

PHYSICS OF STRENGTH

From chapter 1 we know that force (F) is equal to an object's mass (M) times its acceleration (A) against gravity (F = M × A). The "against gravity" refers to the fact that to overcome the effect of gravity on an object, one must produce at least enough force that is equal to the mass of the object and the acceleration of gravity. For example, to jump we need to produce a force that is greater than our body weight times the acceleration of gravity. The greater the force we produce and the faster we produce it, the higher we jump. As a muscle contracts, it produces rotational force called torque. The force is rotational because the bone moves through an arc within the joint's specific range of motion. Because an arc is created, it is nearly impossible for a single joint to create movement in a straight line. However, the most effective way to produce pure force is in a straight line. The saying "the shortest distance from one point to another is a straight line" is especially true when lifting a weight. Producing force and keeping the distance short is the name of the game. Thus, short people have a better mechanical advantage and tend to do better lifting weights when compared by body weight. However, that does not mean that a taller person cannot get quite strong.

The key to strength is moving the weight in as close to a straight line as possible and to keep the force of the lift moving in the intended direction. If you produce force outside the object's intended path, that force is wasted. For example, when bench pressing, if force is channeled inappropriately such as extraneous leg and buttock movement, the overall force directed into the bar is reduced. Therefore, correct bench press position uses the legs to exert force upward into the bar.

Moving an object in a straight line when your body is made of levers moving in arcs is trickier than most people think. Therefore, great strength requires coordinating body segments to work together to produce force in a straight line. Practicing a particular movement and using proper technique are the keys to success. To move an object, you must overcome its inertia; this requires great force to initiate movement. It can be accomplished in one of two ways. You can produce force rapidly, or you can apply force for a prolonged time (keep pushing).

PROPER POSITIONING

Gravity causes an object or a person to exert force downward. To be successful in moving an object or person, you must direct your force in a way that will move the object upward and prevent rotational force (torque). To do this, you must focus on body alignment during the movement. For example, when performing squats, although the hips and knees rotate through various arcs in different planes in order to keep the bar traveling upward in a straight line, the force is always directed upward. This means that you need to change the way you do the movement so that force is produced in a straight line, rather than change the line of force to match your body. By concentrating on technique we teach the body to produce optimally, rather than to let the resistance control us.

The following exercises, the big three, are common in most true strength training routines. Because powerlifters are the strongest athletes, we examine the lifts important to their programs and their execution. Although specific modifications can be made to these lifts during your training, the body position and rep execution are designed to minimize the distance the bar must travel and reduce the forces not directed to the bar. These lifts are designed to improve strength in the entire body and may not specifically address the nuances of your particular sport. Once your strength is sufficient, you should modify these lifts to meet your needs.

King of All Exercises: Deep Squat

The squat is considered the king because of the tremendous demand it places on the body. Ask most fitness experts and they will tell you that without the squat you will never make the gains you want. Because of the complexity of the lift, you must carefully follow the steps to squat correctly.

The squat requires great discipline to keep the body in alignment. This exercise is unlike any other in that virtually every muscle in the body contributes at some point during the lift. For strength, this exercise builds a solid foundation in the hips and knees. As a strength exercise, it is often considered the foundation or core exercise and is a staple of nearly every program.

The key to building strength in all lower-body movements is to perform the movements as deeply as possible to increase the range of motion. If that causes too much stress on the knees, limit the range of motion to a level you can tolerate. Not only do these movements develop the desired shape in these specific muscles, but they also increase speed and strength in all lower-body activities. Strong muscles around the hip also decrease the possibility of fracturing the hip and developing hip-related orthopedic problems.

a

b

Deep Squat

Begin by grasping the bar in a closed grip with the palms facing forward; hands are slightly wider than shoulder width. Next, step under the bar and position the feet parallel to one another. Balance the bar on the shoulders in either a *low bar position*, which places the bar across the posterior deltoids at the middle of the trapezius, or a *high bar position*, which places the bar above the posterior deltoids at the base of the neck. Next, lift the bar off the rack, straighten the legs, and hold the chest up and out (*a*). Pull the shoulder blades toward each other while tilting the head slightly upward. Lift the elbows to create a shelf for the bar. Take one or two steps backward and position the feet even with one another and shoulder-width apart. Point the toes slightly outward (*b*).

To begin the next stage of the lift, slightly tilt the head upward to focus on a point 12 to 24 inches above eye level. Slowly and under control, lower the bar by flexing at the hips and knees. Initiate the movement by moving the hips out and back as if to sit on a seat. Keep the body erect. Throughout the lift keep the weight centered over the middle and heels of the feet, not the toes. This keeps the heels on the floor. Keep the knees aligned over the feet. When the tops of the thighs are parallel to the floor, the descent phase is complete (c).

At the bottom of the lift do not bounce with the legs to start the ascent phase of the movement. Initiate the beginning drive by moving the hips forward rather than by extending the knees. Slowly raise the bar by straightening the hips and knees. Maintain proper body position, as described above, throughout the ascent phase. People have a tendency to pinch the knees in. Do not let them move in or out; instead, keep them aligned over the feet. The ascent phase is completed when the legs are completely extended.

c

Squats are typically considered the best exercise for producing overall strength in the hips and knees. Since power is force times velocity (or strength times speed), the strength gained from squatting heavy weights will need to be converted to explosive power. Once an athlete has mastered the exercise, she can work on making the squat movement more explosive. Because the squat movement is similar to jumping, many expect that being able to squat with a lot of weight will translate into a great jump height. However, as we've already learned, power requires speed. Therefore, squat strength alone does not greatly improve jumping height. Chapter 6, Speed and Strength Through Running Drills, and chapter 7, Speed and Strength Through Plyometrics, explain this concept in detail.

Because the basic movement of the squat requires force from the hips and knees working together, all movements derived from hip and knee extension will benefit from squat training. Therefore, the squat is the foundation for all hip-, leg-, and torso-related exercises and movements. Squatting for strength builds the base for power training.

Squat training will develop power when the squat movement is combined with efficient eccentric loading mechanics and reduced ground contact time. Not only is it important to extend forcefully, it is also important to absorb rapidly and convert the absorbed downward force energy to a forceful contraction.

Variations of the squat provide a unique challenge. Many of the exercises to produce power are variations of the basic squat. When it is all said and done, squats are still king. Although many exercises address various aspects of lower-body development, very few can match the intensity that true deep squats bring to the table. Why? Because they provide the optimal combination of downward and upward movement while balancing weight on the back, which requires a combination of skill, strength, and balance. Improvements to the strength of the surrounding hip musculature and developing strong torso strength are added benefits that few other single exercises (meaning needing more than one) can achieve. These variations address muscles such as the abductors (tensor fascia latae, gluteus medius), adductors (adductor magnus, brevis), and rotators of the hip and serve to strengthen movement patterns that might otherwise cause groin and hip injuries.

True-Strength Squat

To squat like a powerlifter, you must rely on hip position. The powerlifter position uses a wider stance with the feet pointed out. This allows the hips to clear on the way to the bottom of the lift. Because powerlifting requires the hips to be lower than the knee at the bottom (the quads are lower than parallel to the ground), flexibility and body position are paramount in attaining depth. The wide stance not only allows depth, but also prevents the knees from pinching in, and coupled with an explosive hip drive, helps the lifter to push through the sticking point. The most distinguishing characteristic of the powerlifter's position is a greater forward lean. If done incorrectly, this exaggerated position can cause excessive pressure on the back. However, if the hips are extended back properly, the bar remains in a perfect line over the heels. This position, along with the strong hip-initiated drive, forces the bar upward in a much straighter line.

Since the squat is such a valuable exercise for developing overall hip and leg strength and power, variations are often built into the training program to help strengthen the groin and outer hip musculature. It is not uncommon in sports for athletes to take lunge-like steps to the side (rather than forward like in a regular lunge) or find themselves in a more narrow stance. Powerlifters use variations of the squat such as narrow (a) and wide (b) stances to develop added strength around the hips. While the wide position may seem excessive, it does help strengthen the inner hip area. Be careful, these are not easy exercises to master! Make sure you keep proper low back form during these movements.

a

b

Bragging Rights: The Big Bench Press

Without a doubt, owning the bragging rights to a huge bench press has its advantages in the weight room. Let's face it, a pile of weight balanced over your neck is impressive. Add to it the ability to lower and raise it without using the legs and it makes it that much more remarkable. However, several skills contribute to the strength necessary for bench pressing a lot of weight, and one of them happens to be incorporating the legs!

The bench press is the best exercise for developing upper-body strength. This lift requires a huge amount of concentration as well as coordination. It forms the foundation for all upper-body pushing movements just as the squat does for the lower body. Developing pushing strength is a relatively simple task from a programming perspective; however, the bench press is one of the most challenging of all exercises. For a tall person, completing the entire range requires a very long pushing force. But even for the shorter-limbed individual, the bench press provides a distinctly difficult challenge.

The bench press remains one of the all-time great lifts and is the basis for almost all strength training programs. To attain great strength in the bench press and its variations it is extremely important to use proper technique.

Bench Press

a

Begin by lying with the back flat on a bench. Place the feet flat on the floor, and keep them flat throughout the lift. The buttocks, shoulders, and head must maintain contact with the bench throughout the lift. With the palms facing up, grasp the bar with a shoulder-width or wider grip. Remove the bar from the rack by pressing upward and extending the arms fully. Inhale deeply to stabilize the upper body (a). To begin the descent phase of the press, slowly and steadily lower the bar to the chest.

Pause a moment when it touches the chest. The bar

should touch a point level with the nipples (*b*).

After the slight pause on the chest, rapidly accelerate the bar off the chest. The bar will take a slightly arched path on its way back to the starting position; however, you should attempt to lift it as straight as possible, with the final position being over the neck. Exhale as the bar passes through the sticking point. The sticking point is usually a few inches from the chest during the ascent phase of the lift. Press until the arms are straight.

b

It is easy to see why the bench press, a pure pushing movement, is considered one of the best exercises for strength improvement. The arm extension and chest adduction are stepping stones for building the strength needed for punching, pushing, and swinging movements. Also, all of the general pushing movements, whether overhead like the military press or straight out in front, benefit from developing strong pectoralis, deltoid, and triceps muscles.

Power in the bench pressing movement is often confused with strength. Weightlifting by itself is not effective for training power even when performing a lift explosively, because much of the lift is spent slowing the bar after it is accelerated before lockout is achieved. In the next chapter, we examine this in greater detail.

True-Strength Bench Press

The powerlifter uses a specific set of movement patterns because the rules of power-lifting state that the head, shoulders, and buttocks must remain in contact with the bench during the entire lift. Because you cannot bend the rules in competition, bench pressers have turned to biomechanics to determine the optimal strength position for maximal bench presses. The optimal position for bench pressing uses a wider-than-shoulder-width grip. When the bar is at the chest, the elbows form an angle of 90 to 100 degrees, and the arms form a 90-degree angle at the armpit. The back is arched, bringing the shoulders and buttocks closer together.

The scapula is retracted to lift the chest higher. The feet are pulled back slightly so that the knees form a sharp angle, allowing the legs to drive force through the ground to stabilize the body and add to the upwardly driving force. Finally, the bar follows the opposite arcing pattern because a top-level bench presser incorporates the latissimus muscles into the movement by pulling the arms in at the initial drive off the chest (*a*). The resulting bar path then follows the opposite arcing pattern. This drive phase helps to accelerate the bar past the sticking point (*b*).

a

b

Pulling for Strength: The Deadlift

The deadlift trains the pulling motion and, along with the bench press and squat, completes the big three. As with the squat and bench press, the complexity of the lift leaves no room for error. Proper technique must be followed to ensure injury-free weight training.

The pulling motion is performed in exercises such as lat pull-downs and seated rows; however, neither of these movements is as similar to sports movement as a true deadlift. Most people assume that the pulling movement increases upper-torso pulling strength. That is true in the case of the seated row. However, a true pull relies heavily on the strength and power produced by the legs. Much to people's surprise, tug of war is a leg strength event. Training pulling movements for sports power and sport strength must involve the legs and the coordinated effort of transferring the power from the legs to the upper body.

For true strength in the upper-body pulling motion, we attempt to lock the legs and work on torso strength. For true power, the pulling motion is not performed by the upper body at all, but rather the power developed by the legs to drive the bar upward, as you see in the clean portion of the clean and jerk.

The deadlift is a strength lifters best test. Nothing exemplifies strength more than lifting an object. There is no better method to train back, leg, and hip strength than the deadlift. The art of deadlifting has produced some of the greatest sport competitions ever seen and some of the most inspiring displays of strength ever witnessed.

The deadlift has two main variations: traditional and sumo style. In the traditional deadlift the feet are positioned about 6 to 12 inches apart. In the sumo-style lift the feet are as far apart as possible without touching the weight. The traditional deadlift requires a much stronger back, and the sumo-style lift is best suited for shorter lifters with stronger hips. The wide stance typically requires the bar to travel a shorter distance, but unlike the other lifts, a taller lifter may benefit from the position achieved with the narrow stance. When the legs are farther apart, the hip and knee interaction can cause awkward mechanics.

Deadlift

Begin by taking a shoulder-width stance with the feet flat on the floor. Grasp the bar with a closed, alternate grip. This grip should be slightly wider than shoulder width. Squat next to the bar with the heels on the floor and the knees inside the arms.

To assume the ready position, start with the arms fully extended. The elbows point out to the sides. Position the bar over the balls of the feet, close to the shins. The shoulders are over or slightly ahead of the bar. Next, establish a flat back posture by pulling the shoulder blades toward each other, holding the chest up and out, and tilting the head slightly up. Focus the eyes ahead or slightly above horizontal. Keep the torso tensed throughout the lift (a).

Begin the pull by straightening the knees. Move the hips forward, and raise the shoulders at the same rate that you extend the knees. Keep the angle of the back constant. Pull the bar straight up, and keep it close to the body throughout the lift. The elbows must remain fully extended. Keep the shoulders back and above or slightly in front of the bar, just like in the ready position (*b*). After the bar has passed the knees, thrust the hips forward and continue pulling until the knees are under the bar. Pull until full knee and hip extension is achieved. At full knee and hip extension, establish an erect body position (*c*).

A variation on this style of deadlift is the sumo-style deadlift. This kind of lift is performed in the same manner as the traditional lift, but the feet are placed in a wide stance (*d*).

a

b

c

d

Great deadlifters are rare. Unlike the bench press and squat, the deadlift has not seen major improvements over the last decade or more. In fact, the most ever lifted is a little more than 930 pounds; the 900-pound barrier was broken in the late 1980s. This lift presents a fundamental problem for levers. Another explanation for the slow improvement is that the equipment for deadlifting is not nearly as effective as the suits for squatting and the shirts for bench pressing.

Whether it is the equipment or not, I believe the main reason for the slow improvement is that the low back plays far too large a role in the overall strength required to perform pulls. And for most, that presents a formidable challenge. Biomechanically speaking, the low back, composed of many vertebrae with their own mechanical issues, and the lack of stability in the midsection seem to prevent the superbig numbers (not that 900 pounds is anything to sneeze at). Perhaps as science peers deeper into the mechanics, the 1,000-pound barrier will be broken. We could see an interesting race between the first 1,000-pound deadlift and the first 1,000-pound bench press.

STICKING POINT

Scientists refer to a weakened leverage point as the *sticking point*. The term must refer to a definite and obvious point, because everyone encounters it, no matter what his or her level of competition or sport (see figure 4.6).

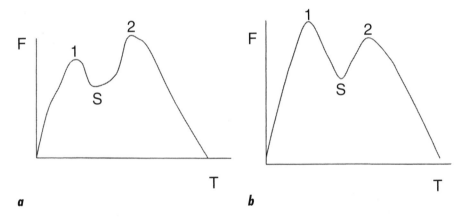

FIGURE 4.6 *Differences between (a) a knee-dominant squatter and (b) a hip-dominant squatter during the concentric portion of a squat.*
F = force output; T = time for concentric portion of lift; 1 = force application before the sticking point (first phase); S = sticking point; 2 = force application after the sticking point

"How do I overcome the sticking point?" I have been asked this question more than 100 times, and have found that my answer disappoints many lifters. Most people are hoping for a brilliant angle-specific answer. But the answer is simply, you don't. You can read thousands of explanations and learn hundreds of lift variations that reduce the sticking point, but unless you are prepared to work hard you will not be able to reduce its effects, and even if you do reduce its effects, each lift will still have a sticking point. No matter who you are, you will inevitably find a precarious position during any lift that affords much frustration. The sad fact is that a sticking point exists in all dynamic movements.

Simply put, your body is a complex system of levers built for speed, not strength. When you try to challenge your body to move an object along a path it doesn't want to take, the body's architecture prevents you from achieving certain things, or at the very least, changes the way you do things. The theory of levers explains why this is true. Let's examine the mechanics of the bench press. The bench press uses primarily the pectoralis major, the anterior deltoids, and the triceps. Although each of these muscles performs different actions at separate joints, the goal is a single effort combining all muscles. As a muscle contracts, it pulls the bone through a path around the joint. Remember, muscles do not push, but pull bones, which creates the pushing action. The joint acts as a pivot point causing a rotational force known as torque. The farther away the lifted object is from the muscle's line of action, the greater the muscular force required to overcome the resistance. This complicated system of moving muscles creates various torques, depending on each muscle's point of origin, point of insertion, shape, size, and line of pull. With all these factors contributing to lifting a barbell, it's not surprising that at some point, competition between opposing muscle groups minimizes the overall production of force. And this is what causes a sticking point. At some point during any movement, the barbell will slow while the muscle fights through the transition of least leverage. The transition means that during any movement there is a point where mechanical advantage is very limited. It occurs where either the least amount of musculature is able to work together or the lever mechanics are not optimal. Thus the lifter will go through this transition. Of course, the more complicated the lift with many joints and muscle groups involved, the more likely a sticking point is to occur. In fact, multiple sticking points may occur. Specifically in the bench press, the dominant muscles are the pecs, triceps, and anterior deltoids. When muscles are stretched optimally (when the bar is at the chest) they have the greatest recoil and produce the greatest force somewhere just after the stretch response (discussed in chapter 7) kicks in. At the chest, the pecs and deltoids are in optimal position. However, the triceps, while active, need the arms to be extended more before they can really get involved. As the bar moves upward, the pecs and especially the deltoids begin to lose some of their force-generating capacity while the triceps are just getting started. Once the bar is far enough off the chest it is a matter of locking the arms and less contribution from the deltoids and pecs are needed. The transition is problematic for those that do not have well-developed strength-generating pecs when the triceps try to join the movement, and for many becomes the sticking point. Others experience the sticking point higher up in the movement when the triceps are not producing enough force.

   The easy solution to overcoming the sticking point is to cheat. Yep, pull the bar right through the sticking point by using some unrelated body part to bypass the most difficult part of the lift. However, you can elevate your butt off the bench only so far, and do only so many CPR compressions and risk cracking your sternum before you finally give up! In fact, cheating merely exacerbates the sticking point problem because you never train the muscles properly to overcome it. Therefore, the first rule for dealing with the sticking point is to use proper technique and form.

   As you have learned, the bar should travel in a line as straight as possible. Rule number two is as follows: Avoid extraneous horizontal bar movement. Although it is true that the bar will follow a slight curvilinear path, the curve should be minimal. The bar's line of force should be directly over the major force line produced by your body. That means that during a bench press, the force should travel down through the wrist, through the forearm to the elbow, and the bar should be parallel to your upper arms when the bar is at the chest during a bench press. Note that bringing your elbows in too close to your body causes the bar to be out of line with the arm. In a squat, your weight should be balanced directly over the heels with the force of movement traveling through the trapezius, legs, and heels during a squat. The final key to overcoming the sticking point is maintaining body stability while on the bench or during any standing movement. Erroneous movement steals from your ability to produce linear force.

   The following are tips for overcoming the sticking point and improving your bench press and other lifts:

   • Dig your shoulders into the bench, and keep your butt on the bench. This allows you to stabilize your shoulder capsule, which minimizes horizontal bar movement and keeps the bar moving upward in a straight line.

   • Wrap your thumb around the bar. Some people believe that a thumbless grip helps isolate specific muscles. However, this makes no difference in muscle activation. In fact, it creates a small amount of extra torque around the wrist because the bar mass does not travel down the forearm.

   • Use your legs in the bench press. Place your feet wide apart to stabilize the body and slightly back to create a sharp ankle angle. As you begin to press the bar up, the contribution from the legs keeps the body tight and forces the buttocks into the bench.

   • Retract your scapula to keep your chest out.

   • During exercises, whether squatting or benching, squeeze your shoulder blades together. This stabilizes the shoulder, but more important, it keeps the body in proper alignment. With squatting and deadlifting it helps keep the torso erect, and with bench pressing it increases the arch in the back and helps activate the lats at the initial drive upward.

OTHER TRAINING TIPS

The following are tips to help improve your lifting abilities:

- Take at least 48 hours between workouts, making sure you are sufficiently recovered from training smaller muscles before attempting big-lift exercises. Doing shoulder work the day before the bench press or calf work before a squat or deadlift day can reduce your ability to produce force.

- Occasionally use pause repetitions in which you completely stop the bar. This forces the muscles to work harder to generate force. It may even help you power your way through the sticking point. Pause repetitions will develop pure strength and acceleration at the bottom portion of the lift, reducing the help from the prestretch, which helps produce force.

- There is no way to truly train portions of a lift. Although many believe that training partials is beneficial, if you cannot get the bar moving out of the bottom of a lift with enough velocity, you will fail at some point. Timing transitions and bounces is difficult and should be avoided. The best way to get through the sticking point is to increase the initial power and drive out of the hole. Training partials does have merit; however, training the entire lift from its starting point is more beneficial. Some people believe that training partials (like lockouts or just pushing off the chest) will help through sticking points. Moreover, it is the ability to produce that extreme force at the bottom that will power through the sticking point.

- The best way to improve the big lifts is to perform hardcore, gut-wrenching, big-lift powerlifting. Go all out and work different grips and wide and narrow foot positions into the program, but keep the motion the same. Various angled pushing movements also complement the main lifts; but remember, this will not alleviate the sticking point. Use dumbbells in your auxiliary exercises to increase the effort of your stabilizers in controlling extraneous weight movement. And most important, use weight you can handle. If the weight's too heavy, willpower won't move it, and you'll just waste your time. Instead, reduce the weight and work the technique and you will improve your chances of beating the sticking point.

- Explode off your chest or out of the "bucket" during a squat, or any exercise. Imagine a stick of dynamite at the beginning of the concentric movement. When the bar touches the chest, or you get to the bottom of the squat, rather than bounce, pause for a moment, then try to ignite the dynamite and drive the bar up past the sticking point.

- Lower the bar slowly. Slowing the bar and controlling the rebound effect at the bottom of the lift takes a lot of energy, but this controlled descent allows the stored energy and the muscles' elastic properties to aid in producing the force for the concentric portion of the lift. Dropping the bar too fast causes the muscles to have to fire to stop the bar. That firing effect loses the additional force-generating capacity that the eccentric portion of the lift helps with. In the case of the bench press, this is where guys bounce it off the chest to gain back that lost energy. It is wiser to bring it down slightly slower, building more of the stored elastic energy.

- In the bench press, the bar should touch across the nipples. Grasp the bar in a wider-than-shoulder-width grip to keep the force moving down through the forearm. In the squat, the bar should be low on the trapezius muscles to maintain proper alignment.

- When bench pressing, take a huge breath and hold it when you lower the bar. This expands the chest, shortening the distance the bar must travel in the bench press, but also increases abdominal-wall strength aiding in overall support during most upright lifts. When you get to the bottom, as you explode the bar upward, forcefully exhale to help power the bar up.

- Shorten the distance the bar travels by improving your overall mechanics. For the deadlift, widen the stance. For the bench press, widen the grip. For the squat, widen the stance and move the bar down on the trapezius muscles.

- Explode out of the bottom of every movement. Rather than trying to move the weight, imagine moving your body away from it. Picture yourself pushing away from the weight in the bench press and away from the floor in the squat. Although this doesn't really happen, it provides a strong mental picture going into the exercise.

Recall from chapter 1 that strength is one of the two major elements of power. Because strength is the ability to exert force, and force is equal to an object's mass times its acceleration (usually against gravity), the stronger we are, the more weight we will move. It is time now to examine how strength interacts with speed. Remember, strength alone is of little use in most sports. Producing force quickly is more useful. Acceleration becomes important. It is not enough to just overcome gravity, but to truly jump high, kick hard, and move fast, we must explode with strength.

5

Developing Explosive Acceleration

Although speed and strength are important to athletes, acceleration, or how quickly a body or an implement's speed increases, is one of the most important aspects of sport. And the faster you can apply force to an object, the faster it will accelerate. The larger and heavier the object, the greater its inertia and the greater the force needed to overcome it. This has been demonstrated time and again through Newton's laws of motion. In terms of sport, let's look at two sumo wrestlers with equal skills. A 500 pounder should have a greater chance of staying in the ring than a 300 pounder because of his increased mass. So why can the 300 pounder occasionally win? Perhaps it has something to do with being able to generate more power. Read on and find out.

To move an object, we must apply sufficient force to overcome its inertia. The object will remain in motion until another force is applied to stop it. In the case of athletics, we must recruit the appropriate muscle fibers and they must contract in the proper sequence to produce force. This force overcomes the object's inertia, and the object begins to move. The faster we recruit the fibers, the faster we can accelerate the object, and the quicker it gets where we want it to go!

Once the object or body is in motion, it has momentum, and unless we continue to exert a force or we change the amount of force or its direction, the only thing that will impede the object's motion is a counterforce such as friction or gravity. Put your car in neutral and give a push. A light push will not move the vehicle, but once you apply enough force to overcome its inertia (the downward force of the tires on the ground) it gets rolling, and then keeping it rolling becomes easier. If you continue pushing, the car keeps moving until you encounter a force greater than the force you are providing, such as the gravity you encounter on a hill. Your car's engine works the same way, with the gas pedal controlling the rate at which you accelerate the car.

In weightlifting, gravity is most often the force that slows or stops momentum. To successfully lift a weight, you must apply continual force to counteract the force of gravity. This is where acceleration or explosive lifting is important. As stated earlier, if you can apply enough force rapidly enough (hmmm, sounds like power) then maybe the bar or the object will travel some distance. For example, in the shot put you only have the time in the ring to transfer force to the shot to make it go the distance you want. Therefore, that force needs to be as large as possible. This illustrates the idea behind power training. If you could continue applying force to the shot during its flight, it could travel an infinite distance. But because you can only apply force over a distance equal to the length of your body (transferring the force from your legs, through your torso, into your arms, and through your fingertips), you must apply as much force as possible as rapidly as possible to propel the shot.

TRAINING FOR EXPLOSIVE POWER

Training for explosive power using weights develops rapid force. However, when undertaking this training it is important to maintain the proper balance between workouts with weighted objects or weights themselves and sport-specific training. Training with weights or a weighted object teaches the neurological system to recruit fibers maximally for that specific task. For example, throwing a heavy ball trains your muscles to recruit the fibers necessary to throw a heavy ball, not to throw a baseball into the strike zone at 90 miles per hour. Using a weighted ball requires a slightly different on–off neurological skill set than throwing a standard ball. Therefore, you must practice the sport-specific movement concurrently with power training to avoid a negative training transfer.

That being said, explosive training using slightly heavier implements produces remarkable results in an athlete's overall power profile. In the case of body-weight movements such as plyometric exercises, the overload stimulus is the weight of the body during the exaggerated eccentric loading. In the case of weightlifting movements such as the power clean and snatch, the weight is relatively heavy, but the lifting technique is what keeps speed at a premium. However, trying to explosively pull heavy weight is a sure way to cause injury if form is broken.

Therefore, your guiding motto is to lift weight within your own capability and use proper progression.

Explosive Power: The Power Clean

The power clean is one of the most common explosive lifts for improving sports performance and many credit this lift with their sports successes. However, no exercise in and of itself can be responsible for improving sports performance. A particular exercise is a valuable training tool only if the athlete can transfer the gain in strength, speed, or power into competition. Although many advocates of the Olympic lifts staunchly believe that these lifts mimic the movements seen on the field or on the court, the correlation between their performance and on-field success has never been measured and is at best a guess. So why do we do this lift?

Power cleans teach the body to recruit hip and leg musculature as rapidly as possible to generate enough force to overcome the bar's inertia. The faster and greater you can apply that force, the faster and stronger you will become. But not because you can lift the weight, rather because you can call the specific muscles involved in hip and knee extension to fire rapidly. Thus, the power clean is a recruitment tool for hip explosion. When looked at that way, you can see its value in building jumping power and driving power in the leg.

As in all lifts, technique is the name of the game. At first glance, the power clean looks like you just rapidly pull a huge weight. However, most pulls are initiated by the legs, and in the case of the power clean, the arms should remain locked during the initial pull, making this truly a hip-dominant exercise. In fact, if the arms and trapezius are too involved in the lift, the benefit of this lift for athletic performance transfer is lost.

In all exercises proper alignment is important, but in lifting weight out in front of the body or overhead, it is even more important. Recall from the discussion on levers that the farther the bar gets away from the body, the greater the counterforce necessary to prevent it from overtaking the lift. Keep the bar close to the body so you don't have to use your low back muscles to counterbalance the weight. Additionally, keep the body rigid, particularly the arms. If the joints are slack, force will dissipate rather than transfer directly from the body to the bar. Some believe the power clean puts athletes at risk for injury. If you perform it correctly, you will remain injury-free and will reap all the benefits it offers.

Power Clean

Begin by placing the bar on the floor so that it is touching the shins. The feet are shoulder-width apart. The head is up, the chest out, and the shoulders back. The back is flat with a slight arch at the base. The ankles, hips, and knees are flexed. Position the shoulders over the bar, with the arms straight. Grasp the bar slightly

a

b

wider than shoulder width with palms facing in. For most athletes, one inch in front of the smooth part of the bar is adequate. Depending on the athlete's flexibility, the grip position might need to be modified slightly for comfort reasons.

Perform this lift as explosively as possible. Begin by rapidly extending the ankles, knees, and hips at the same time. This timing is very important, and a common flaw is extending the hips first, making the movement essentially a straight-leg deadlift. As the legs approach full extension, powerfully shrug the trapezius muscles. Also, as the legs approach full extension, powerfully pull the elbows up, while keeping them over the bar. As the body becomes fully extended, extend the ankles (*a*).

After the bar reaches sternum level and the body is fully extended, rapidly lower the body under the bar. Rotate the elbows forward, extend the wrists, and slightly raise the shoulders to cushion the bar landing on the shoulders. After the bar is caught on the shoulders, accelerate the body out of the bottom position. Once the bar has started upward, thrust the hips forward so that they are under the bar. When the body has passed through the sticking point, exhale through the mouth. Keep the muscles of the torso contracted throughout the ascent phase of the lift. Lock the knees (*b*).

After achieving a standing position, a controlled drop is recommended to return the bar back to the floor.

Speed and Power: The Power Snatch

This is by far the fastest, most explosive lift in all of weight training. Because of its unique nature, this lift has garnered special attention in the world of strength training and in the Olympic Games. As its name implies, speed is necessary for proper performance. Remember that the power clean requires explosive hip action to get the bar moving, and the snatch requires even more. The tricky aspect of the snatch is timing. The ability to generate enough force to raise a bar weighing 400 pounds or more over a person's head is an amazing feat. And stopping the bar at the top of the movement is just as amazing. Most people believe that the arms and shoulders stop the weight at the top. But this could not be further from the truth. In fact, a true Olympic lifter knows almost immediately after the pull if the lift will be successful, because with this exercise, the bar's momentum is timed perfectly to stop overhead. The lifter pulls himself or herself under the bar against the force of the bar moving up. So rather than stopping the weight as people assume, the bar decelerates in such a way that the downward movement of the body against the upward movement of the bar stops it. And the shoulders exert almost no force against the bar to stop it.

Properly executing this exercise requires extreme discipline, tremendous explosion, and cat-like reflexes. Like the clean, if done properly with the bar close to the body and movement generated through hip drive, this lift is an effective tool for developing athletic power.

Power Snatch

Like in the power clean, begin by placing the bar on the floor so that it touches the shins. Grasp the bar with the palms facing in. The feet are shoulder-width apart. The head is up, the chest out, and the shoulders back. The back is flat with a slight arch at the base. The ankles, hips, and knees are flexed. Position the shoulders over the bar with the arms straight (*a*).

The movement of this lift is similar to that of the power clean. Perform the beginning phase as explosively as possible. Rapidly extending the ankles, knees, and hips at the same time is very important. A common flaw

a

is extending the hips first, making the movement essentially a straight-leg deadlift. As the legs approach full extension, powerfully shrug the trapezius muscles and powerfully pull the elbows up, keeping them over the bar. As the body becomes fully extended, extend the ankles (*b*).

The catch is the most difficult part of this lift and takes lots of practice before the lifter feels entirely comfortable with it. After the bar reaches sternum level and the body is fully extended, rapidly lower the body under the bar. Next, rotate the elbows forward and push up against the bar. Fully extend the arms so that the wrist, arm, and shoulder form a straight line (*c*). After the arms are fully extended, accelerate the body out of the bottom position. Once the bar has started upward, thrust the hips forward to place them under the bar. When the body has passed through the sticking point, exhale through the mouth. Keep the muscles of the torso contracted throughout the ascent phase of the lift. Lock the knees.

After achieving a standing position, a controlled drop is recommended to return the bar back to the floor.

b

c

LIFTING PROGRESSIONS AND SUPPORT EXERCISES

A progression of support exercises can help you learn the complicated movements of the Olympic lifts. The exercises that follow will truly develop proper technique, speed, and power.

Deadlift

Begin the motion with the hips down, chest out, and head up. Pull through the entire motion while keeping the bar as close to the body as possible. Move the hips up and in throughout the range of motion. Do not initiate the lift by extending the knees or the low back. Although there are two styles of deadlifts, sumo and traditional, use the close-stance traditional lift when teaching the progression of the power clean and snatch. Rather than the alternating grip, use the power clean grip with both hands pronated. The breathing pattern for this exercise is the same as in all lifts: Exhale through the sticking point of the upward movement and inhale during the downward movement. Note here that unlike the deadlift in chapter 4, both hands need to face in the same direction (that of the clean and snatch) if this is used as a progression for these lifts rather than just a deadlift.

High-Pull

Position the bar on blocks or in a power rack so that the bar is at midthigh level. Grasp the bar in either a clean or snatch grip, depending on which lift you're learning. The head is up, chest is out, and shoulders are back. The back is flat with a slight arch at the base, and the feet are shoulder-width apart. Flex the ankles, hips, and knees. Position the shoulders over the bar, with the arms straight.

Begin by rapidly extending the ankles, knees, and hips. As the legs approach full extension, powerfully shrug the trapezius muscles and powerfully pull the elbows up, keeping them over the bar. As the body becomes fully extended, extend the ankles. Your goal should be to pull the bar up to or slightly higher than sternum level.

To finish the movement, lower the bar and straighten the elbows until the bar is back to thigh level. After the bar returns to thigh level, flex the ankles, hips, and knees to return the bar to the blocks.

Push Press

Begin by placing the bar in a squat rack or power rack. Grasp the bar with an overhand grip. Step under the bar with both feet, and position the bar on the shoulders. Lift the bar from the rack and take a few small steps back. The head is up, the chest out, and the feet shoulder-width apart.

Initiate the movement by flexing the ankles, hips, and knees slightly so that the body descends about four inches. Rapidly extend the hips, knees, and the ankles until the body is fully extended. After reaching full extension, quickly press the bar in front of the face (*a*) and overhead. The movement is finished when the arms are locked (*b*).

To lower the weight back to the starting position, bend the elbows and in a controlled manner, lower the weight onto the shoulders. As the weight approaches the shoulders, slightly bend the hips and knees to cushion the weight.

The snatch press is a variation of the push press. It is performed the identical way with the only variation being in the grip placement. To measure optimal grip for the snatch, extend one arm laterally so that it is parallel to the floor. The other arm hangs down the side of the body. Measure the distance from the outside of the shoulder of the arm that is hanging to the knuckles of the closed fist of the

a
b

arm that is extended. The distance measured is the proper distance that the index fingers should be placed from one another while grasping the bar. An important tip to keep in mind is that the push of the bar overhead must begin in conjunction with the end of the explosive extension of the legs.

Push Jerk and Split Press

The split press is a variation of the push jerk. While performing the catch phase of the push jerk, the feet remain shoulder-width apart. In the split press, the feet split apart from one another while the bar moves upward. It doesn't matter which foot goes forward, the athlete should do whatever is most comfortable. The feet should land between 24 and 30 inches apart.

a

b

Overhead Squat

The overhead squat begins with the bar at the highest point in a squat rack or power rack. The hands are positioned on the bar with the snatch grip, however the clean grip variation is also acceptable. Keep the head up and the chest out. The shoulders are back, and the back is flat with a slight arch at the base. The feet are shoulder-width apart or slightly wider, and the toes point out at an angle of 30 to 35 degrees.

Accelerate the body out of the bottom position. Press the bar overhead, inhale deeply, and contract the muscles of the torso to help stabilize the upper body. Once the bar has started upward, thrust the hips forward to place them under the bar (*a*). When the body has passed through the sticking point, exhale through the mouth.

Keep the feet flat on the ground, and initiate the descent by slowly lowering the buttocks toward the floor. Descend until the tops of the thighs are slightly past parallel with the floor. Keep the head up and chest out, maintaining a neutral spine position throughout the lift (*b*).

Olympic Lifts As a Power Training Tool

After reading this, you no doubt feel you must put these exercises into your training program. Be careful! No exercise is a "must do." These exercises themselves will not make you faster or more explosive, or for that matter, make you a better football, basketball, or hockey player. In fact, they could be counterproductive if you do not execute them properly or integrate them correctly into your training program. Lots of practice is the only way to perfect these lifts and make them a viable training tool. However, don't let the fact that it takes a while to learn these explosive lifts keep you from trying them. If you are interested only in quick results, you will no doubt sell yourself short in all aspects of your training. As you already know, there is no quick and easy way to athletic success. Explosive lifting is no exception. A progressive coach or athlete with a good program will work these lifts into her program over time.

This leads to another problem: time. If you're a coach, do you have enough time to properly supervise these lifts? If you're an athlete, do you have enough time to devote the number of hours necessary to master these lifts so that you can execute them properly? I have witnessed dozens of high school and collegiate athletes improperly perform these lifts under the assumption that the lift alone makes the athlete better. An Olympic lifter spends years perfecting the movement. He starts the process by using a broomstick! So why is it that you can walk into a typical high school or college strength room and see athletes performing these lifts incorrectly? Time. Most coaches do not take the time to properly teach the biomechanical principles and techniques necessary to develop power through these lifts. Instead, they pitch the exercise into the training program because they are supposed to. If you do not have time to properly teach and supervise a lift, don't include it in your training program. In fact, many successful world champions in explosive events have never used these lifts. They are of little value if they are not performed properly.

Coaches who have successfully implemented explosive lifts into their programs have done so using proper progressions and integrating them over a relatively long period during the off-season when the athletes had time to perfect the lifts. It's interesting to note that opponents of explosive lifts tout their dangers and ignore their advantages, claiming that they take too long to perfect. Yet these same coaches spend hours, days, and months trying to execute specific plays and perfecting sport-specific technique. So why won't they take the same time to teach power-improving exercises?

Would you allow a basketball player to shoot jump shots without squaring himself to the basket? Would you allow a baseball player to raise his bat at the end of his swing or a golfer to ignore her follow-through? Of course not, you would correct their technique and help them learn to recruit the appropriate muscle fibers to do the work. As coaches, we work and rework a movement until it is perfected. We should do the same in our power training programs. We need to incorporate explosive lifts, but we need to do it correctly, taking sufficient time to do so. So why do we allow our football, basketball, tennis, hockey, and baseball players to lift improperly? It makes no sense. If you want to truly learn to develop the Olympic lifts as a power training tool, I recommend purchasing a book and video about Olympic lifting.

Explosive Release Movements With Traditional Resistance

Most strength coaches and exercise scientists believe that success in nearly any sport is determined by an athlete's ability to generate power. The latest information indicates that working muscles must contract at high speeds if power is the goal of the training program. Yet high-speed training has a clear limitation when performed in a resistance training environment. In any training movement with a discernable endpoint, the athlete must decelerate the bar before it reaches the end of the range of motion. Some believe this premature deceleration reduces the effectiveness of high-speed training, because it interferes with power production during the functional part of the movement. For example, if you were to try to accelerate a barbell as fast as possible in the bench press with a less than maximal weight to continue producing power, the barbell would leave your hands (setting yourself up for a potentially ugly ending). If you were to try to stop it from leaving your hands, you would have to slow it back down. To do this you would either have to have a hearty set of brakes in the chest or reduce the power you generate off your chest at the beginning. Either way, that is not beneficial as that would be like stopping a volleyball spike or baseball bat right after contact—meaning no follow-through. And that is just the problem; explosive weightlifting has no follow-through or time to decelerate the bar after maximal power is developed. Clearly, high-speed training is necessary, and using resistance makes sense because power is the combination of speed and strength. The trick is to find a safe way to combine both. Coaches and scientists have come up with a few solutions. Although some are slightly beyond the budget of many high school strength rooms, several alternatives such as release moves using medicine balls are discussed in chapter 7. Release movements, where the resistance, once accelerated can be let go, are best for producing power. Hence, the use of medicine balls and other weighted implements are common in power training routines.

Many athletes practice ballistic activities, such as weighted depth jumps and squat jumps in an attempt to reduce the deceleration effect and maximize power development. But other athletes avoid these movements because they carry a high potential for injury if the athlete is attempting to control a high-speed external weight. This is especially important in high-speed power movements, such as the bench press, where the bar must be released if you want to avoid the deceleration stage. Of course, releasing the barbell has serious disadvantages if it cannot be caught on its way back down and there are few devices capable of doing this (hence the next points and the upcoming chapters).

But avoiding explosive movements in training may not be the best strategy if your sport requires explosive activity. Although safety is an important issue, you must find ways to train your body to withstand the rigors of sport. Just because an exercise may present a safety concern does not mean you shouldn't attempt it. Rather you should approach the exercise with a plan for proper progression. Start with light weight and make sure you build a strong base and are strong enough to properly control the weight.

Another option for safely developing speed is equipment that catches a barbell upon release. Several future-busting companies are designing equipment that does just that. Several companies have developed specialized equipment to produce power more optimally for position-specific athletes. Companies such as CORMAX have developed machines that allow the coach to control the speed of the descent after the weight reaches its maximum height by tightening or loosening a knob. Others, like ProSpot, are designing equipment that moves in multiple planes while catching the weight after it is released (*a* and *b*). In my own laboratory we are working with these two companies to examine the efficacy of release throws and jumps. Our research shows force curves that are much longer and reach greater peaks than those traditionally seen in regular explosive resistance training. We have been able to show that when a barbell can be released, superior force and power are produced.

a   *b*

Additionally, we have also seen that the angle at which max force and power are achieved is slightly different than when the bar is held. This has led us to believe that perhaps our training methodologies should be altered. For example, in the previous chapter we saw how strength athletes, in particular powerlifters, are required to perform exercises in a specific fashion (achieve a specific squat depth). With release power movements as seen in typical sporting activities such as kicking, throwing, and tackling through someone, we see that angle specificity may be an important factor. Returning to the squat, some powerlifters will mock a person who does not squat to the deep-bucket position. Therefore, many strength coaches who are former lifters require their athletes to go to full-squat depth (otherwise it is just a half lift). However, a typical football lineman never squats to a deep position during a game, and if you look at tape of a lineman pushing, you will see that his knee angle is nowhere near parallel! Are our linemen squatting too deeply in the weight room? Should we use shorter sport-specific angles for developing power? While it is too early to tell, we certainly need to open our minds to the distinct possibility that half squats may produce power better suited to the needs of some games and events. And therefore, we should vary the depth according to the needs of each position within a sport. Take the same squat example and apply it to a baseball catcher who spends a lot of time in a deep crouch, but must explode upward to throw a runner out at second. Although the appropriateness of tailoring power lifts to the needs of specific sports is up for debate and our research is trying to find answers, it sure opens the door for some fancy training programs.

Sticking Point Again

Some suggest that during the squat movement, emphasis shifts from a hip drive to a knee drive as the angle of leg flexion increases during the concentric portion of the lift. Hip dominance in power production is vital because far greater force and power can be produced when the larger hip extensor muscles are more involved. Research has shown that more skilled lifters produce more force at various points during squatting, and those hip angles and knee angles interact strongly. The powerlifter uses more hip power and leans over farther than less experienced lifters, who use a more upright position. And more experienced lifters create peak force and power output at the initial drive starting the concentric movement. This shows the superiority in producing power rapidly at the bottom portion (beginning of the concentric phase) of most lifts. What is most striking about this research is that the advanced lifters not only squat more deeply, but also produce far greater force throughout the entire lift, even when lifting the same weight as the other lifters. Thus, it is clear that power production is the key element, and when using lighter weight, there may be angle-specific implications. Finally, the greater the overall power produced, the smaller the amount of power and force required to get past the sticking point.

The following sections describe how to perform explosive bench presses and squats. When done safely, these exercises can form the bulk of the power phase of your training program.

Power Bench Throw

The execution of the power bench throw is much like a regular bench press or incline press. The difference is that this lift does not stop at full extension, rather it accelerates through the entire lift and the barbell, dumbbell, or medicine ball is released from the hands. Of course to do an explosive throw, you must have the ability to safely release the weight (as with special equipment or medicine balls). As the weight descends (eccentric), the lifter builds up stored energy (which will be explained in the next chapter). The stored energy is converted to force when the positive (concentric) portion of the lift begins. The lifter explodes the bar off the chest, continuing the driving phase as long as she can. At lighter loads, the lifter accelerates the bar through the sticking point. At heavier loads, the sticking point is more obvious. Interestingly, even at very light loads, lifters experience sticking points, albeit quite small.

At the lighter loads, the acceleration and force should cause the bar to release earlier than the heavier loads. In either case, the bar accelerates much longer than if you tried to explode a regular plate-loaded barbell upward (do not try to release a barbell in this position if you are not using specialized catch equipment). Another thing to remember, do not bounce the bar off the chest in an attempt to develop more power (you could get hurt, and CPR-like compressions with the bar are not the name of the game with this lift). The key to building explosive power is maintaining control, and like in the Olympic lifts, you must control the bar or object.

Power Squat Jump

In this exercise, the squat movement is similar to a regular squat, and the explosive component is similar to a vertical jump. As the athlete descends with the weight, he or she controls the rate of descent to properly time the "bounce" at the bottom. Actually, it is not really a bounce, but a recoil, transition, and conversion to maximal upward effort performed at the bottom of the lift. The distance the athlete should descend is governed by the angles necessary for the sport. Recall our discussion about deep squatting. The research my colleague and I are doing and others have done indicates that squat depth should be dictated by the requirements of the sport. The speed with which stored energy can be converted is the key to athletic success. The longer the eccentric phase, the more energy is stored; however, if that energy cannot be converted quickly, much of the force production will be lost. Therefore, use light weight with these lifts. In the case of the specialized equipment, we are able to release the weight. If you are unable to release the weight, landing during power squat jumps should be done cautiously. Remember to bend the legs when landing to absorb the shock and compressive effects of the weight on your back. Finally, during these lifts, explode and continue to apply the upward force for as long as possible. Doing either of these lifts with half effort is fruitless.

Once you've trained the muscles necessary for explosive acceleration, it's time to concentrate on speed. The next chapter discusses the role of sport speed in the power equation.

6

Speed and Strength Through Running Drills

Some strength coaches have suggested that speed and strength are developed concurrently, while others say that one depends on the other. Either way, most agree that an athlete must possess the strength to produce force at the rapid pace today's sports require.

Creating optimal speed depends on an athlete's ability to combine speed and strength. Recall that maximal speed is at one end of the speed–strength continuum. In the past, most coaches and athletes assumed that only sprint speed could be trained and improved effectively, and that the speed to swing a bat or spike a volleyball relied more on natural ability. Innovative coaches have begun to train rotational speed and foot, hand, and eye speed in addition to running speed.

In this chapter we will explain and train for two kinds of speed. The most often trained is *straight-line* or sprint speed. However, most important for an athlete is *sport speed.* An athlete's impressive straight-line speed may not be valuable to her team if she cannot convert it to sport-specific movements. With the exception of track events, few sports rely on straight-line running. Instead, a combination of agility and quickness is required. These are the main components of sport speed. Conditioning is also integral to sport speed. A very fast athlete who tires quickly will not be able to use her speed in the final period or last few minutes of a game. At this point, the better-conditioned athlete may outperform the faster athlete. Therefore, not only must you become faster, but you must also be able to call upon your speed when you need it, even when you are exhausted.

It is also important not to confuse speed with conditioning. Improving speed and using it to develop power should be undertaken separately from conditioning and endurance training.

Locating your sport's speed requirement on the speed–strength continuum is necessary for developing a precise training protocol. As discussed in chapter 1, sports that require pure speed are those that involve throwing, swinging, or kicking and end with a follow-through motion. But most sports require speed at various intensities depending on the play or sequence of movements. Most sports are clustered around the speed-strength portion of the continuum. Refer to table 1.1 on page 13 in chapter 1 to see where your sport fits on the speed–strength continuum. Once you have determined how much your sport relies on speed or speed-strength, you can determine the proper balance between straight-line running and the sport-speed drills for agility and quickness. Sports that are mostly speed-strength should employ a variety of drills for both straight-line running and sport speed. In sports where the emphasis is on power or strength-speed, sport-speed drills should be employed more often. For sports at the speed end of the continuum, it is usually best to spend time on rotational drills rather than speed drills; however, in speed training, the emphasis should be placed on sport speed. And pure-strength athletes will do best with straight-line sprints and lateral shuffles where quick directional change is not usually a priority. See table 6.1 for more details on choosing speed training for your sport.

Table 6.1   Choosing Speed Training

	Speed	Speed-strength	Explosive power	Strength-speed	Strength
Relative speed training %	20–30	40–50	20–30	20–30	5–10
Straight line %	20	50	40	30	80
Sport speed %*	80	50	60	70	20

The first row in this table represents the relative percent of speed training versus other training modalities. The following rows show the percent of straight-line versus sport-speed training time spent doing specific drills by speed-strength classification.

*In pure-sprinting track events, very little time is spent working sport speed.

When using table 6.1, you must make sure your sport can truly benefit from a specific form of training. For example, in golf, where there is no foot movement (during the swing), it would be pointless to spend time doing agilities and straight-line sprinting.

STRAIGHT-LINE SPEED

Speed training is vital for increasing an athlete's chances of success. Coaches spend a lot of time teaching running form drills, start technique, acceleration drills, and stride-mechanics drills to increase straight-line speed. However, because these drills are technique oriented, they take time to perfect, which makes proper progression important. The athlete must gradually learn the movement, which is best accomplished at a slower teaching speed. However, once the athlete has mastered the technique at a slow speed, he can integrate it into the speed program by executing it quickly. The purpose of form drills is to teach proper stride mechanics, not increase speed, although a more efficient stride is usually a quicker stride. Just like with weightlifting exercises, don't be tempted to practice so many that you can't master any of them, thereby losing the speed training advantage. Remember, unless you are training a track athlete, you are not training your athlete to be a sprinter; your time may be better spent working on other training components (this is the same notion as we are not training our athletes to be weightlifters, merely using weightlifting to help improve performance).

Proper straight-line speed training should emphasize a few properly executed drills, progressively increasing the speed, then perfecting the movements at top speed before introducing additional drills. You will develop the necessary skills over time, while seeing immediate gains such as improved coordination and balance in some areas. Begin with drills that train the most general movements and progress to the most specific. Start with the least complicated exercises and progress to the most complicated. Less complicated exercises are ones that involve just a few joints such as practicing arm action or leg cycling, whereas more complex drills involve synchronizing arm and leg action together such as acceleration sprints. In general, determine the number of sets and reps according to your ability to perform the exercise properly at the desired intensity. Straight-line speed drills can be used for interval training.

Breaking down a movement into its basic components helps you understand how to execute the movement. Running uses hundreds of muscles, not only in the lower body, but also the upper body. In fact, strengthening the upper body increases the power and speed of the running stride. The arm swing propels the body and stabilizes it. The running motion uses nearly every muscle of the lower body. To produce a running stride, both flexion and extension occur at the hip, knee, and ankle. In addition, the joints of the feet at the tarsals, metatarsals, and phalanges also work. At each of these joints several pairs of muscles work in sequence to produce movement. Although we've all been running since childhood and take it for granted, it is perhaps one of the most complex movements we perform.

Two components contribute to running speed. Stride frequency refers to the number of times the leg cycles through the running movement per unit of time. Stride length is the distance covered by each stride. The force of the foot's contact with the ground and the ability to rapidly absorb the body's impact and turn the force around are part of the phase known as the push-off phase. The resulting force that propels the athlete forward is directly related to the force into the ground and the duration the foot remains in contact with the ground. The push-off phase affects stride frequency and stride length. You can see how complex the running motion is by looking at just one leg cycle. The leg accelerates as it pushes off the ground, maintains speed as it cycles through, and decelerates before the foot strikes the ground. This incredible process occurs in less than .2 seconds for an elite-level athlete. The drills described in this chapter can help you increase stride frequency, the power of each push-off, stride length, and the speed of the cycling movement.

The faster you can stride—increasing the number of foot contacts and decreasing the amount of time the foot spends on the ground—the faster your legs will turn over and the faster you'll cover ground. This can be done by being pulled or assisted or running downhill; in either case, your legs are forced to turn over quicker. When running downhill, choose a hill with a grade of 7 percent or less; otherwise, you will gain too much speed, making it hard to control your stride, putting you at risk for injury. The method for increasing stride frequency is to run on a flat surface concentrating on increasing the number of strides by using specific devices and drills that make leg turnover more efficient.

Resistive running, running uphill, running up steps, and bounding drills can help increase stride length. However, a stride that is too long, like a stride that is too short, will decrease your speed. Optimal stride length varies from individual to individual. Therefore, very fast athletes should not necessarily attempt to change their running pattern by altering stride length. When working on stride mechanics, you will relearn the movement by perfecting neurological timing and body control.

There are two ways to increase stride length and frequency. One is to increase the strength or amount of force the running muscles produce. The other is to improve the mechanics of the running motion. Both are related. Increasing muscle strength will help produce a more forceful contraction, which will increase the distance of the stride by increasing the push-off strength. This gain in strength will also make it easier for the athlete to pull her legs through a straight path, driving her knees forward, and perform other movements efficiently as she works on drills to improve mechanics. The key is to continue regular running drills in conjunction with resistive and hill running.

Resistive running is key because the athlete must produce greater force to propel himself forward, backward, or laterally. Resistance can be in the form of specialized stretch tubing, a parachute or sled, or by simply slowing the athlete down by holding on to his waist belt or standing in front of him. When using a device such as a chute, it is important to help "set the chute" by throwing it up so that it catches air and provides adequate resistance. If you are using someone else to provide resistance, be sure that he does not interfere with the athlete's leg turnover or body position.

Additionally, release-resistive running has also proven effective for training break-away speed and first-step quickness. To do this, simply set up the resistance device so that it can be released by using either a Velcro attachment, or just completely releasing the cord. Be careful when releasing stretch tubing as it will snap back and hit the runner or tangle in his legs impeding running performance. It is best to release by throwing the tube toward the runner.

Running Form Drills

Coaches rely on technique or form drills to develop speed. The goal is to perfect arm motion and push-off strength. To generate force from the hips where the running stride begins, concentrate on snapping the thigh down. To help do this, it is common for coaches to tell the athletes to try to drive the foot forcefully into the ground, while concentrating on leg and arm motion. Form running drills are not necessarily specific to running in that most drills exhibit leg movements that are not exactly run-like. However, from a sport-speed standpoint, if done correctly and quickly, the form drills can help increase speed or at the very least, increase footwork. Be careful not to spend too much time trying to change an athlete's running technique, especially in sports where true straight-line running is limited. Form drills certainly help improve stride mechanics, but when training time is limited, the focus should be on developing strength and power for the overall running movement. For most non-track athletes, form drills are incorporated into the general warm-up and mechanics are emphasized during the strength and speed drills.

Common form drills are As and Bs, high-knee drills, and variations of heel-kick drills. If an athlete cannot perfect these movements, drop the drills from the program. Although these activities are common in practice sessions for most sports, research into their ability to increase sport-specific speed is lacking. However, because most running coaches are convinced of their ability to train speed, other coaches believe it's likely that their benefits carry over to other sports. Incorporate these drills into your program if time permits.

Generally, straight-line speed training should be performed with relatively long rest periods to allow for maximum power production. The emphasis should be on the adenosine triphosphate and creatine phosphate phosphagen (ATP-CP) system to prevent lactic acid accumulation and early fatigue. Practicing the drills without sufficient rest reduces your ability to perform the drills at maximum speed. If you can't perform the drills maximally, the technique is compromised and the

MY FAVORITE WARM-UP

This warm-up is beneficial and helps coaches reduce time spent on drills. I have found many coaches are using this same type of warm-up sequence.

If you are looking to develop straight-line speed, then the focus of your training should certainly be on form, technique, and acceleration drills. However, for most sports, since straight-line running is only a small component, it may make more sense to incorporate form running drills into your warm-up and then focus on specific agility and quickness drills. Remember, warm-ups are an important part of training and if you are coaching each repetition, the athlete can get great benefit from including running technique into your general warm-up. The following warm-up drill sequence will help the athlete perfect his or her running technique.

Position field markers about 20 yards (18.29 meters) apart and perform the following sequence of running and stretching movements. Be certain to pay close attention to technique during each drill. At each marker the athlete will perform a stretch. When moving between markers (M1 and M2), the athlete will do a running-technique (RT) drill.

1. From M1: Light jog to M2
2. At M2: Hamstring-low back stretch (bend over and touch ground)
3. From M2: Fast feet (max reps per yard)
4. At M1: Three position ham-back stretch (legs wide—bend to middle then sides)
5. From M1: Butt-kickers
6. At M2: Quad stretch
7. From M2: Ham-kickers
8. At M1: Groin stretch
9. From M1: A-skips
10. At M2: Hip flexor stretch (lunge position—stretch back leg)
11. From M2: B-skips
12. At M1: Trunk rotations
13. From M1: Lateral shuffle
14. At M2: Partner chest stretch
15. From M2: Carioca steps
16. At M1: Partner upper-back stretch
17. From M1: Acceleration sprint
18. At M2: Squat jumps (plyometric warm-up)
19. From M2: Sprint to M1

ability of the drill to increase straight-line speed is diminished. Each drill should be performed full out, with a rest interval equal to 12 times the work period. Remember, a five- to six-second sprint (which is way adequate for most sports) is asking for one to one-and-one-half minutes of rest (that is not unreasonable). For most drills the distance should be 20 to 40 yards and the athlete should stop and rest. For certain sports, however, you may want to perform repetitive bouts with less rest, to mimic the competition environment and anaerobic lactic acid system better. For example, as you are nearing the football season, drills should last 3 to 7 seconds, with rest lasting 20 to 30 seconds (play to in-between play interval). For tennis, drills should last 3 to 6 seconds and rest should be about 15 to 30 seconds (play from service and time before next service).

SPORT SPEED

Sport speed transfers straight-line speed into skills useable in your particular sport. Many athletes can run a fast 40-, 60-, or 100-yard dash, but often they can only exhibit this speed if they are open. Although these athletes may have excellent stride mechanics, their acceleration, agility, quickness, or strength may not be adequate to free themselves from their opponents and really open up. For example, a wide receiver in football with a very fast 40 or 100 time may be held up at the line of scrimmage by the defender if he cannot use his speed to break away. A lack of strength or agility hampers his sport speed. Furthermore, running downfield while looking back at the quarterback or making a cut or move to get open and then catching the ball on the run is very different from straight-line running. Lack of fitness also limits sport speed. For example, if, as the game progresses, the wide receiver becomes tired as he works against his opponent, he may not be fit enough to make the big play even if he does get open.

In order for an athlete to be successful, she must be able to use her speed during competition. Not only must she be fast, but also be in good condition. Therefore, sport speed should be trained according to the sport's physical demands, movement patterns, and energy system requirements. In the case of soccer, speed training should teach the basic elements by working on the technique of stride mechanics and sprint training then incorporate the technique into an anaerobic and aerobic conditioning program. Drills may be more straight-line oriented from a moving start to simulate the constant movement of the game. In the case of football, powerful speed movements should be incorporated into an anaerobic alactic and anaerobic lactic training program. Alactic refers to drills lasting up to 10 to 15 seconds with long breaks where lactic training would include short drills that may last up to 30 seconds but the rest time would be much shorter, not allowing lactic acid to clear and phosphagens to replenish. Drills may incorporate starting against resistance or making a first move prior to the straight-line sprint. In both cases, the rest-to-work ratio should be equivalent to the demands of the sport.

When training for speed, spend more time on conditioning of speed as it relates to your sport. This means for a tennis player that speed should be developed in short bursts with minimal rest time (similar to the rest between points) and for a soccer player, increasing speed within the aerobic realm (meaning sprint, jog, sprint, jog, etc.) than on increasing straight-line speed. Often conditioning coaches concentrate on increasing speed so that their athletes will perform well on speed tests (this may be important if an athlete trying to move to the next level requires a certain test score to be accepted into a program or onto a team); that is not as important as developing the athlete's speed for his or her sport. Sport-speed drills may be the same as straight-line drills but performed with less rest, or they may more closely resemble the movements specific to a particular sport. The combination of movements in agility drills may limit their ability to train speed, but they will improve your ability to start, stop, and change direction, and eventually increase the speed at which you can perform these movements.

Agility

Sport speed is affected by the athlete's ability to rapidly shift direction. If an athlete cannot change direction and regain speed, he or she will not be successful. Quickly changing direction requires precise footwork and the ability to accelerate rapidly after the direction change. Athletes most often run into problems when switching from backpedaling to forward running. An athlete with good footwork and acceleration can backpedal longer and more quickly, giving himself more time to react to a play's movement.

Crossover footwork drills are important to most sport training. In fact, in sports where athletes must cover a relatively short direction, direction change itself may be the limiting factor. For example, a baseball player leading off at first base has a better chance of stealing second if he can execute a good first crossover step. Because the player starts out facing the pitcher, the initial quick crossover step may be the difference between a stolen base and an out. Because the distance between bases is 90 feet (30 yards) and a player takes about a 10- to 15-foot lead (3 to 5 yards), there is not much room for straight-line running, especially if the player slides for the last 3 to 5 feet. Therefore, footwork is the key to success. With many other sports, the movement pattern starts defensively (looking out for the play), then switches to offensive (heading to the play). Therefore, the direction change followed by the immediate acceleration is usually the determining factor. Drills that are designed to increase sport speed should begin with a rapid direction change followed by 10 to 30 yards of acceleration. However, very short drills with rapid direction changes develop overall footwork, balance, and coordination. These drills help athletes in contact sports learn how to adjust to awkward positions after being pushed or jostled.

SPORT "READY" POSITION

The ready position is often referred to as the sport position. It is a position that favors both rapid movement execution and the ability to become more stable. For rapid execution, you need to be able to see the play develop, react quickly, and have proper body position to make the first movement. In order to gain stability, you must be able to drop down to lower your center of gravity and widen your base of support quickly. The sport ready position allows you to do this. Proper sport position is standing with your weight on the balls of your feet with knees and waist slightly bent. Keep your chest and head up and your arms relaxed, slightly bent, and slightly out in front of your body.

Practice and perfect several individual major cutting moves before attempting more complex drills. A cut is a specific action taken at each cone. For example, when running up to a cone, your cut could follow a sharp or rounded path or include a complete stop followed by a 180-degree turn and a backward movement. Initially, work on controlling your body position during each of these movements. The following exercises train the cutting moves.

Stop and Back

Place two cones 10 yards apart. Start at one cone and sprint to the second. Come to a complete stop in a sport ready position (*a*). Quickly turn and accelerate back to the first cone, sprinting past the starting point (*b*). Focus on maintaining balance over the feet and changing directions as quickly as possible.

a

b

Stop and back.

90-Degree Round

Set up two cones about five yards apart. Start at one cone and sprint to the other. As you get close to the second cone (*a*) slow slightly and make a 90-degree turn, then accelerate past the cone (*b*). When rounding the cone, stay as close to it as possible, maintain an athletic position, and take short, choppy steps. Shift your body weight slightly over the inside foot.

a

b

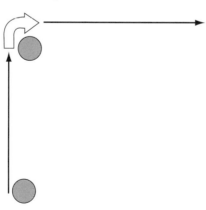

90-degree round.

90-Degree Cut

Set up two cones five yards apart. Start at one and sprint to the other. As you get to the second cone, drop into a sport ready position (*a*), then make a sharp lateral cut and accelerate past the cone (*b*).

a   *b*

90-degree cut.

180-Degree Turn

Set up two cones five yards apart. Start at one cone and sprint toward the other (*a*). At the second cone make a 180-degree turn using short, choppy steps, then accelerate back through the starting point (*b*).

a   *b*

180-degree turn.

360-Degree Turn

Set up three cones five yards apart. Sprint from the first cone to the second (a). At the second cone make a 360-degree turn, running around the second cone using short, choppy steps, keeping your body weight shifted slightly over the inside foot (b). Sprint out of the turn past the third cone (c).

a   b   c

360-degree turn.

After the athlete has mastered the cutting moves, you can begin work on the specific movement patterns illustrated in the following diagram. Each drill trains the ability to change direction and features one of the basic steps: crossover (a), angled backward run (b), backpedal (c), shuffle (d), or sidestep before sprinting in a straight line. In each drill you perform the required step from A to B, then sprint straight to C. Focus on the footwork, the directional change, and the first few steps in the sprint. Place cones A and B about 7 to 10 yards apart and cone C about 15 to 20 yards away from B. To train sport speed, perform sets of repetitions with a short rest interval. You can combine individual drills to create additional drills. Because these exercises are not complicated, you can learn them quickly. When creating agility drills it is nearly impossible to simulate game-like conditions. But that's OK. The goal of an agility drill is to stimulate foot–eye coordination and to improve the ability to accelerate through changes of direction.

Once you have mastered the cutting moves and learned the general stepping patterns, you can move to more complex drills. Remember, more complex does not necessarily mean better. But these drills will take more concentration and induce fatigue more quickly.

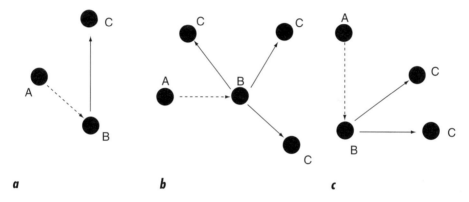

a   b   c

(a) Crossover angle, (b) sidestep and sprint, and (c) backpedal and sprint.

a

b

c

d

Double Box

Set up six cones to form two boxes side by side. One athlete starts in the center of each box. The athlete reacts to a coach's instruction. The coach points to a cone and the athlete sprints to that cone, touches it, then moves back to the center of the square.

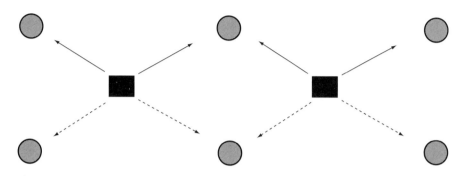

Double box.

Linear Zig-Zag

Set up two rows of three or four cones, with about five yards between each cone. Stagger the rows. Start at one end of the cones, facing the other row. The object is to face the same direction throughout the entire drill. Sprint forward to the end of the line, making tight turns at each cone. Once you reach the end, backpedal through the same course, again making tight turns at each cone.

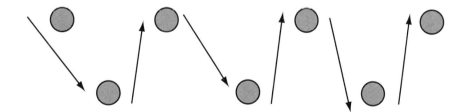

Linear zig-zag.

In agility drills, a set is one complete drill, and each rep is a cut or movement at a cone; one set might include five to eight cone movements. Use table 6.2 to help you to determine your training volume. Quantities are given for workouts consisting of agility drills only (AO) or workouts in which the drills will be included in your regular training routine (TR). The training volume depends on your ability to properly execute the drills. If you can perform them well and with speed, keep it going. Note: The table is a guideline. As long as each rep is still maximal effort, a very well-conditioned athlete may be able to perform more. Not that more is better, but if technique is solid, then it certainly won't hurt.

Table 6.2   Training Volumes for Agility Drills

Athlete's level	Basic movement drills (sets)	Sports movement drills (sets)	Complex drills (sets)
Beginner AO	20	10	
Beginner TR	6	4	
Intermediate AO	10	10	10
Intermediate TR	4	4	4
Advanced AO	4	10	16
Advanced TR		4	8

Strength and Stride Frequency

Drills that improve stride push-off strength and stride frequency can help you develop strength while improving speed. Your focus should be on perfecting the movement patterns that relate to your sport. Not only are these drills fun, but practicing basic stride mechanics with resistance, which makes movement more difficult, or assistance, which causes the legs to turn over more quickly, often yields significant training results. While direct transfer of training to performance is difficult, specific drills that concentrate on phases of a movement do help develop better muscle patterns and improved neural activation. Again, the key here is to practice your sport-skills while you are trying to build power.

Sprint With Partner Resistance

Pair two athletes of comparable speed. One athlete, wearing a resistance belt with rubber tubing attached, lines up in front of the other. The athlete in back provides resistance by holding the rubber tubing as the first athlete begins running. When the tubing is taut, the trailing athlete starts running. The trailing athlete should maintain constant tension on the tubes without overstretching them. The drill should cover 15 to 30 yards.

Sprint With Partner Assistance

This drill builds off the previous one and is slightly more advanced. Pair two athletes, one a little faster than the other. Follow the same procedure described for the partner resistance drill; however, both athletes start running at the same time. The leader, who is faster, pulls the partner. Maintain good mechanics throughout the drill.

Backward Run With Resistance

Pair two athletes of comparable speed. One athlete, wearing a resistance belt, lines up in front of the other. The athlete in back provides resistance by holding the rubber tubing attached to the belt as the first athlete begins running backward. When the tubing is taut, the trailing athlete starts running. The trailing athlete should maintain constant tension on the tubes without overstretching them. The drill should cover 15 to 30 yards.

Backward Run With 180-Degree Turn to Sprint

Follow the same procedure as a backward run with resistance drill, but make a 180-degree turn at about 10 yards during the drill and break into a sprint for 10 to 15 more yards (*a*, *b*, and *c*).

a

b

c

Lateral Shuffle With Partner Resistance

Line up two athletes side by side. The second athlete provides resistance for the first by holding the tubing of the resistance belt as the first athlete shuffles 10 to 20 feet to the side. The second athlete can stay in one place or continue to shuffle over the distance, moving with the first athlete. Remember, the tubing should be taut.

Lateral Shuffle With Partner Assistance

Line up two athletes side by side. The second athlete assists the first by using the resistance belt. The drill should cover 10 to 20 yards. This drill helps athletes experience what it feels like to move laterally at maximal speed.

Forward Acceleration

This drill uses a resistive device such as a power chute or sled. Start from a modified sprint start with one leg back and one hand on the ground. Sprint forward, taking short steps at the start and gradually increasing stride length over the first 10 to 12 strides. The trunk should stay inclined for the first three to five steps, then gradually raise. When the coach releases the chute for this drill and the others, he or she should toss it into the air so that it opens quickly.

Backward Acceleration

Again, as in the forward acceleration drill, the athlete will need a chute, sled, or resistive device. Start with the feet hip-width apart, knees slightly bent, and trunk inclined forward. The toe of one foot should be aligned with the heel of the other. While facing straight ahead and keeping the shoulders square, backpedal on the toes. Start with short strides, gradually lengthening the stride for 15 to 30 yards.

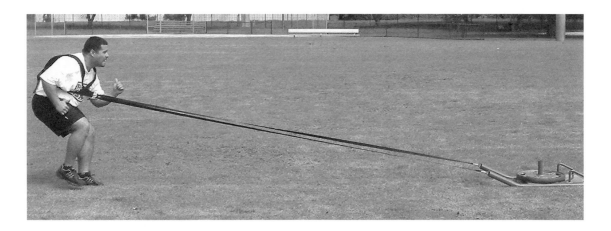

Forward Run

From a standing start sprint as quickly as possible for 30 yards. Forcefully drive the arms forward and backward. The arms should not swing across the body. Lift the knees so that the thighs are parallel to the ground at the top of each stride. After 30 yards, decelerate gradually. This drill and all of the following five drills can be done with two parachutes to increase the resistance.

An alternative to this drill is to perform the same movement backward.

Backward Run

Start with the feet hip-width apart, knees slightly bent, and trunk inclined forward. The toe of one foot should be aligned with the heel of the other. While facing straight ahead and keeping the shoulders square, backpedal with long strides. Pump the arms forward and backward. Keep the shoulders over the feet, with the knees and waist bent. Quickly extend and flex the hip to create quick turnover.

Lateral Crossover to Sprint

Start with the feet shoulder-width apart, knees bent, waist slightly bent, shoulders over the feet, and weight on the front half of the foot (*a*). During the crossover step, turn the hips. Drive the trail knee across so that the thigh is parallel to the ground. Turn both knees and feet into the direction you are traveling. The hips rotate, but the shoulders should rotate very little during the crossover step. A partner provides resistance (holding a chute, belt, etc.) during the crossover step to help develop hip extensor and flexor strength (*b*).

a

b

Zig-Zag Forward Run

Start as you would for the forward run (*a*). Place a series of cones about three yards apart in a pattern similar to the linear zig-zag drill on page 123. Cut around the cones as quickly as possible (*b*). The drill finishes with a 10-yard straight run (*c*). The type of cut is determined by the amount of wind. On a very windy day you will be able to make sharp cuts and keep the chute open. On a calm day or if you're doing the drills inside, you will need to make wide, rounded cuts to prevent the chute from folding. This drill can be done with many different resistive devices.

a

b

c

This drill can also be done with a backward variation. Start with the feet hip-width apart, knees slightly bent, and trunk inclined forward. The toe of one foot should be aligned with the heel of the other. Facing straight ahead with the shoulders square, start backpedaling with long strides, pumping the arms forward and backward. Keep the shoulders over the feet, with the knees and waist bent. Quickly extend and flex the hips to create quick turnover. Run backward, following a zig-zag pattern. The cut around the cones will be determined by the amount of wind. On a very windy day you will be able to make sharp cuts and keep the chute open. On a calm day or if you're doing the drills inside, you will need to make wide, rounded cuts to prevent the chute from folding.

Forward Sprint With Release

Wearing a chute (or sled), start as you would for the forward run. Start sprinting; after 10 yards unfasten the chute's belt by pulling the Velcro, letting the chute fall to the ground behind you. Continue to sprint for another 10 yards. You should feel an increase in speed after losing the chute.

Backward Run Into a Turn and Sprint

Attach a parachute or sled loosely around the waist with the chute or sled in front. Start with the feet hip-width apart, knees slightly bent, and trunk inclined forward. The toe of one foot should be aligned with the heel of the other. Facing straight ahead, keep the shoulders square and start backpedaling with long strides, pumping the arms forward and backward. Keep the shoulders over the feet, with the knees and waist bent. Quickly extend and flex the hips to create quick turnover (a). After 10 yards, quickly spin (b) and sprint forward (c). If the belt is loose enough, you should be able to spin within the belt so that the chute is now behind you as you sprint forward.

a

b

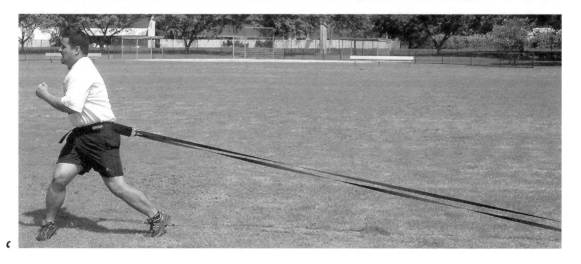

c

Quickness

Quickness can be described as first-step speed. The speed developed within the first few steps produces a quick action, which is powerful or explosive. Acceleration is also a key element of quickness. Being quick is probably the best measure of an athlete's ability to use his speed. An athlete who can quickly get where he needs to be is more valuable than an athlete with the best sprint time. This is because most sport actions occur over very short distances limited by the size of the field, court, or arena.

Quickness is hard to train because it encompasses reaction time and skill. A quick athlete usually has good peripheral awareness. She knows where to go and how to turn on the jets to get there. By developing agility and practicing reaction drills, you can develop quickness. A good method for developing quickness for sport is to perform the movement pattern drills described earlier, but make point B, rather than C, the reaction point (as shown in the sprint, cut, react drill). When you reach point B, throw, kick, or pass a ball toward point C or to some other spot your coach points at. However, you won't know where point C is until you reach point B.

Top-end speed is only truly sport specific if you can reach the top end within the first 10 yards. If you can run 100 yards lightning fast, but need 40 yards to accelerate to top speed, you will not get the chance to use your speed effectively. The athlete who can accelerate in 10 to 15 yards will prevail, especially when the play itself only covers 10 to 20 yards. Reaction, agility, and first-step explosion combine to form quickness.

Another key component of quickness is how quickly you can move your legs or feet. A quick athlete maintains proper body position and gets his feet into position rapidly. One of the best ways to train this type of quickness is to use specific footwork drills. These can be achieved by using speed ladders, dot mats, and line drills. In particular, ladder drills have a specific purpose—to improve foot speed. You have heard of hand–eye coordination, well how about foot–eye coordination? Simply put, your ability to make your feet go where you want, when you want is the key ingredient in first-step foot speed. The challenge with ladders is to perfect an unnatural movement by forcing the feet to go in a specific spot. Balance and coordination are integral in movement, because not only is it necessary in sport to get to the point of attack, but you need to be in control of your body for the next movement. Ladder training does just that. It makes you place your feet quickly and trains your balance at the same time. When creating drills (and there are hundreds of variations), the goal is to make the step pattern specific and challenging. Note that there is no such thing as a sport-specific step pattern, rather, that the athlete must move the way the drill is designed. Once the athlete masters the step pattern, he or she should increase speed of execution. Once top drill speed is attained, and technique is perfect and no ladder spaces are missed, then it is time for a more challenging drill. When teaching ladder progressions, it is recommended to walk through the drill and have the athlete slowly increase speed. There is only one other thing to think about. If you want to be successful at sport, you must keep focused on the ball or your opponent, and that is hard to do with your eyes looking at the ground. So you must be able to complete drills without looking down often for this type of training to be useful. This added dimension makes progression a key element in the development of ladder drills. The remaining drills in this chapter include ladders and cones to focus on footwork.

Front and Back and Shuffle (With Reaction)

Set up three cones five yards apart from each other in a straight line. Start at the middle cone. On the coach's command, backpedal, run forward or backward, or shuffle to the cones indicated by the coach.

Front and back and shuffle (with reaction).

Sprint, Cut, React

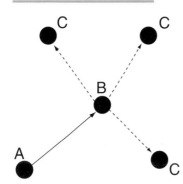

Set up the cones as indicated in the figure (five to seven yards apart from each other). Begin by standing at cone A. Sprint forward to cone B, then cut and sprint to one of three cones depending on the coach's instructions.

Sprint, cut, react.

Ladder Quick Feet

Start at one end of a ladder, facing it. Begin by stepping into the first box with the right foot. As soon as the right foot touches the ground, step into the same box with the left foot. Continue until you reach the end of the ladder. Repeat the drill with the other foot leading.

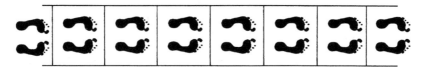

Ladder quick feet.

Ladder Sidestep

Stand at one end of a ladder, with the ladder to your left (*a*). With the left foot, step to the side into the first box as close to the second rung as possible. As soon as the left foot touches the ground, step into the same box with the right foot (*b*). Continue until you've reached the end of the ladder. Repeat the drill to the right.

a

b

Ladder sidestep.

Ladder Hop

Start at one end of the ladder, facing it with the feet together. Hop from one box to the next as quickly as possible (*a* and *b*). You can also do this drill by hopping sideways from one end of the ladder to the other.

a

b

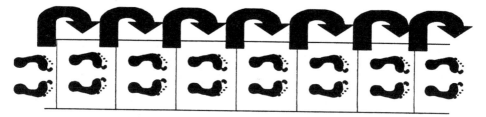

Ladder hop.

The Boxer

Start on the outside of the ladder on the right or left side, facing the ladder. Using a scissor-like motion, put the right foot in the first box (*a*) followed by the left foot in the second box (*b*). The next step is to advance the right foot to the outside of the ladder (*c*) followed by the left foot.

a

b

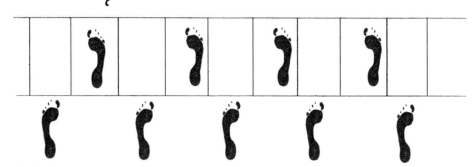

c

The boxer.

Icky Shuffle

Begin with the left foot in the first box and the right foot next to it outside the ladder. Bring the right foot into the first box. Then, with the left foot, step up to the outside of the next box. Bring the right foot directly into the next box, then bring the left foot into the box with the right foot. Repeat this process with the right foot leading the next step.

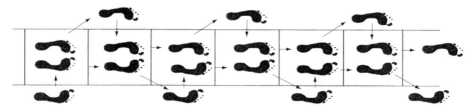

Icky shuffle.

Hurdle Run

Place a series of hurdles two feet from each other in a straight line. Hurdles can be set up to 12 inches high. Run in a straight line over the hurdles, placing one foot between each hurdle. Drive the knees high for maximal hip flexion. Keep the elbows at 90 degrees, driving them forward and back. Keep the head up and eyes forward throughout the drill.

For a variation, perform the movements backward. Just as in the forward hurdle run, place a series of hurdles two feet from each other in a straight line. Start with your back to the hurdles and backpedal over the hurdles, placing one foot between each hurdle. The nose should remain over the toes of the foot that's in contact with the ground. Make sure you pick your legs up high enough. This drill will feel very awkward at first. Arm action should be pumping, but again with this drill it is particularly difficult to move the arms properly.

Hurdle Side Shuffle

Place a series of hurdles two feet from each other in a straight line. Start with your side to the first hurdle (*a*) and step sideways over it. As soon as the first foot is planted, step over with the other foot (*b* and *c*). Maintain a sport ready position as you move through the drill. Maintain efficient arm action by keeping the elbows at 90 degrees, driving them back and forth as you raise each leg. Keep the head up and eyes forward throughout the drill.

a

b

c

Hurdle Zig-Zag Shuffle

Set up the hurdles in a zig-zag pattern. Shuffle through the hurdle course making quick 90-degree turns at each hurdle. Keep the hips and shoulders parallel to each hurdle (*a*, *b*, and *c*).

a

b

c

In general, these running hurdle drills, where jumping is not the goal, improve leg turnover and sport speed. These drills should have movements where foot–ground contact is short and speed through the hurdle set is rapid. These drills can be performed forward, backward, and laterally and should employ about 10 to 12 hurdles. Ensure proper body position is maintained, eyes are focused on the direction you are traveling, and arm action is consistent with leg movement for maximal speed.

These quickness drills teach you to carry momentum into your sprint. To make the drills sport specific, change the starting stance. Incorporate these drills into your regular training program or do them on a speed or agility day. Because the purpose of these drills is to teach you how to quickly move your feet where you want them to go, they should be done explosively. Training these drills when fatigued is fine if the purpose is conditioning, but to improve overall quickness, these drills should be done when you are fresh, with lots of time between sets to recover. Table 6.3 breaks down the number of quickness drills athletes at various levels should do.

Table 6.3 Quickness Drills

Athlete's level	Quickness training only (sets)	Quickness with other training (sets)
Beginner	12–15	8
Intermediate	20	10
Advanced	30	15

It's clear that being fast is vital to athletic success. But you can add one more tool to your athletic toolbox: acceleration, or the rate at which you increase speed. Since most movements in sport happen rapidly in response to a reaction, and there is little time to get to the point of attack or to beat an opponent, your ability to out accelerate an opponent means reaching the ball before she does in soccer, for example. Acceleration is the force produced after the first step (quickness) is taken. Acceleration and technique are the keys to an explosive sprint start or change in speed from either a moving or stationary position. Transferring momentum from one type of movement, such as a crossover step, to a straight sprint is crucial to developing speed you can use.

Another method for combining speed and strength is plyometric exercises. The next chapter discusses how to use plyometrics to produce power you can use in sport.

7

Speed and Strength Through Plyometrics

Power—a combination of speed and strength—is required for nearly all athletic movements. Jumping, bounding, and hopping exercises have long been used to enhance power and improve athletic performance. These exercises develop an explosive reaction through powerful muscular contractions as a result of rapid eccentric contractions. In recent years, this distinct training method has been termed plyometrics.

PLYOMETRIC TRAINING

Plyometric exercises serve the same purpose as strength training: They develop physical power and quickness. Some athletes spend huge amounts of time in the weight room trying to increase power with barbell and dumbbell exercises.

Although weight training has its place, it is not the most efficient means of developing power. Traditional weight room exercises do not allow the athlete to move quickly enough or use the movements needed to develop sport-specific power.

Mechanics Behind Plyometrics

Speed and strength are directly affected by a muscle's fiber type (fast or slow twitch), the speed of the muscle contraction, and the speed and efficiency of neuromuscular firing. Plyometric training is the key to improving these three muscle characteristics. Plyometric exercises train both fast- and slow-twitch muscle fibers. Certainly power work has a greater effect on fast-twitch fibers over slow-twitch fibers; however, forcing slow-twitch aerobic fibers to contract faster will improve their firing capability as well. By improving contractile and recruitment rate, greater force can be produced more rapidly and therefore improve the power of muscle action.

Specific training induces change to all fibers be it under aerobic or anaerobic conditions. However, it does not increase the number of fibers nor completely convert fibers. Training (again not just power but all training) forces fibers to take on the characteristics of the muscle fiber type that are most common with the sport. For example, sprinters over time force their slow-twitch fibers to adjust to a more rapid firing rate. The change is not immediate and may take several years before adaptation occurs—that is why sprinters continue to get faster to a point.

Although strength training can create the muscular and nervous system adaptations necessary to develop power, plyometrics helps the muscle produce greater force by causing it to rapidly produce that force. Most sport actions, and movements in general, use some kind of prestretch before movement. In fact, prestretch may even be innate. For example, ask a friend to stand still, then tell her to move rapidly sideways in the direction you point. Watch her closely. The first move she makes will be a small and quick shift to the opposite side, then she will move in the direction indicated. This movement is no coincidence; the prestretch helps propel the person to the side faster.

How and why do your muscles react to prestretch? The answer is complex, and because the effect occurs within milliseconds, it is imperative to understand the process to ensure that you attain maximum benefit and maximum safety. A muscle has two kinds of sensors, one within the muscle belly, called the muscle spindle, and the other within the tendon of the muscle, called the Golgi tendon organ (GTO).

Muscle Spindle

The muscle spindle lies deep within the muscle belly along the fibers. It registers and sends information about the stretch and length of the muscle to the spinal cord. When it detects a severe or rapid stretch, it sends a message, and the return message tells the muscle to contract. While the muscle spindle is telling the muscle to contract, it undergoes a process known as reciprocal inhibition, which tells the opposite (antagonistic) muscle not to resist the agonist muscle's contraction process. This is best illustrated by the ol' knee cap whack at the doctor's office. When the patellar tendon is tapped, the quadriceps muscle rapidly stretches (in this case a small movement), which in turn registers with the muscle spindles causing the quadriceps to contract, causing the lower leg to rise rapidly while the hamstrings release from contracting (reciprocal inhibition).

Golgi Tendon Organ (GTO)

The golgi tendon organ (GTO) registers changes in tension and stretch within the tendon. This defensive sensory mechanism helps protect the muscle by sending a signal when tension becomes too great. The signal tells the muscle to stop contracting and causes the opposite (antagonist) muscle to contract. This stops or holds the movement (like an isometric hold) or slows it. Unlike the signal of the muscle spindle, which tells the same muscle to contract, the GTO signal stops the muscle contraction. An example would be trying to curl a very heavy dumbbell (greater than your 1RM). You would begin to move it, then the biceps would just relax (tension was too great). In this case, because the resistance was so great, the effect of gravity would pull the weight back down and the triceps (the antagonist) would not have to contract. Some scientists and coaches believe that reducing the action of the GTO and its effect on the contracting muscle would allow greater tension to develop and possibly greater gains in strength. In fact, advocates practice reducing the GTO effect in strength training and in stretching and flexibility training. In strength training, it is done by overloading the muscle at various positions along the movement. An example would be bench pressing in a safety rack and setting the rack height at a position off the chest. The lifter will push a light-loaded bar against it (making it isometric) creating maximal tension for 5 to 10 seconds. In flexibility training, the lifter would stretch to a close-to-maximal range, then force the muscle to contract with as much force as possible by either pressing against some form of resistance or immovable object (isometric). These are not easy ways to train, nor are they advised for athletes in or near their season, or without a solid resistance training background.

Elastic Energy

A third concept in plyometrics is called elastic energy. When a muscle undergoes a prestretch, it begins to build up energy. If released promptly (as in the pulling back on a rubber band and releasing it) this energy aids muscle contraction. However, if the muscle is stretched and held too long, it will not produce an explosive effect, and in fact it will have to work even harder to do the same work. To illustrate, try this with a partner: Do a single complete bench press repetition with a moderate to heavy weight, starting with the arms fully extended and lowering the bar to the chest. This is an eccentric contraction. Pressing the bar back to the start is a concentric contraction. Next, start with your hands at your chest receiving the bar from your partner. Now, give it a push. I'll bet this rep with the identical weight is considerably harder. This also explains why the first rep in a dumbbell press is always the hardest. Generally, when using dumbbells, you start with the concentric portion of the lift. For example, dumbbells start on shoulders for a shoulder press. Almost all barbell exercises start with the eccentric portion, and machine exercises usually start with the concentric. During the eccentric movement, the nervous system has time to tell the brain how much weight is there, how much stretch is occurring, and how much counterforce is required for the concentric movement. This eccentric contraction allows the GTOs and muscle spindles to do their jobs. In a purely concentric movement, there is no elastic energy buildup nor a stretch for the receptors to monitor. In the case of the bench press exercise, without the eccentric contraction, your muscles did not experience a prestretch, and therefore gained no elastic advantage.

Although it has not been entirely proven, it is likely that plyometric movements can increase strength by reducing the inhibitory nature of the GTO and muscle spindle. Through proper training, it may be possible to decrease the GTO's effect while increasing the muscle spindle's ability to help execute rapid movements.

Plyometric Components

Three main components of a plyometric movement are the eccentric action, amortization phase, and concentric action. The eccentric component is where the initial prestretch or countermovement occurs. It is the process that stores the potential energy for the ensuing movement. The amortization phase, as the name implies, is the time in which the potential energy is converted to kinetic energy, or movement, or the time it takes to repay the debt incurred by the energy buildup. In the case of jumping, it represents the period between eccentric and concentric contractions when the takeoff foot is in contact with the ground. Upper-body plyometrics work the exact same way except we describe the action in terms of the time a ball or object is in contact with the hand. The concentric movement is the final force created to propel a person or implement upward or forward. If the amortization phase is long, the force required for movement is greater, diminishing the elastic effect of the potential energy stored. The contraction should happen immediately once you have reached the prestretch or countermovement max point. Again using the bench press as an example, impose a three-second pause at your chest before pushing the weights. With the elastic energy all but gone, this movement becomes much harder. This is illustrated in figure 7.1.

Figure 7.1 shows how rapidly the loss in force output occurs. Within .3 seconds of an imposed pause (this includes reaction time of approximately .2 to .4 seconds), substantial force-generating capacity is lost. A pause of .7 or more seconds could reduce force output by as much as 30 percent, which could be catastrophic in terms of performance. Further, when this is transferred to power development, a pause of 1 second or more could reduce power by more than 50 percent in maximal effort. If you relate this to plyometrics, a long amortization period decreases the prestretch force-generating effect.

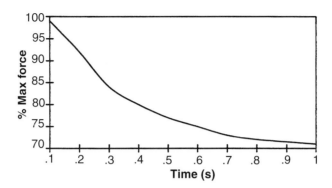

FIGURE 7.1 *Relationship between force output and the amortization phase.*

CONCENTRIC-ONLY ACTIONS

Recall from chapter 2 on testing that we discussed both static vertical jumps (SVJ) and countermovement vertical jumps (CVJ). In the CVJ, we took advantage of the stretch response to perform the movement. If you were to apply this concept to everyday activities, movement would be both slow and very inefficient. To truly understand the value of the eccentric action prior to executing a movement, a simple weight room example illustrates it well. Sit down at a seated bench press and load up a heavy weight that you can do for a few reps. How hard is that first rep? The next few are easier until you finally fatigue. Why? That first rep is a concentric-only repetition. There was no preload, no time for the body to register the weight, and no prestretch to enhance force output. While concentric-only training is often employed as a means for developing muscle strength, in real life and especially sporting movements, we almost always precede the concentric with an eccentric action. Further, by reducing the time between actions, provided the movement is controlled, it is executed with greater force.

Plyometric Sequence

Plyometric exercises always follow the same specific sequence:

Landing phase or loading phase
Amortization phase
Takeoff phase

The landing phase starts as soon as the muscles begin an eccentric contraction. The rapid eccentric contraction stretches the elastic component of the muscle and activates the stretch reflex. Eccentric strength is needed during the landing phase. Inadequate strength results in a slower stretch and a weaker activation of the stretch reflex.

The amortization phase, the time on the ground, is the most important part of a plyometric exercise. It represents the turnaround time from landing to take-off and is crucial for power development. If the amortization phase is too long, the stretch reflex is lost and there is no plyometric effect.

The loading and turnaround contraction time is essential for power development. If you spend too much time absorbing the impact, either because the force is too great or your balance is set off, you will need more time to recover, increasing the amortization time and decreasing force output (figure 7.1 illustrates this). Examples include jumping off a box that is too tall because it takes more time to land, and receiving a fast thrown ball because it takes more time to control. Essentially, the plyometric activity asks you to stop one movement and completely send it back in opposite direction.

The takeoff phase is the concentric contraction that follows the landing. The stored elastic energy increases jump height.

TYPES OF PLYOMETRICS

Plyometrics are typically divided into two categories: single-response drills and multiple-response drills. Within each category are various levels of intensity.

Single-Response Drills

Single-response jumps involve one explosive effort. Because the emphasis is on maximal effort and power in each repetition, there is a rest period between each repetition. After landing, pause to reset the starting position and focus for the next effort. Single-response drills are normally done in short sets (see chapter 3) to avoid fatigue and maintain speed and power.

Jumping in place is the simplest form of plyometrics. This requires little equipment and helps beginners develop jumping skills before they attempt to jump onto or over obstacles. The athlete can jump with either one or two legs.

Standing jumps stress maximal effort in vertical and horizontal directions. These exercises should be done with maximal effort for one repetition, but may be repeated several times. Standing jumps are most often done onto or over boxes, hurdles, or other obstacles. Box jumps are performed by jumping for height on or over boxes or benches from a single- or double-leg takeoff. Hurdle jumps are performed by jumping for height over hurdles from a single- or double-leg takeoff.

Depth jumps are performed by falling or jumping from a height, followed by an immediate rebound upward. Determining the appropriate box height is crucial in a drop-jump program. If the boxes are too low, there will be no overload effect on the muscle, and jump improvements will be minimal. On the other hand, if the boxes are too high, the athlete will have to absorb so much impact that he will lose the rebound effect of the landing.

Box height can be determined by a simple test. Perform a maximum vertical jump (see the section on countermovement vertical jumps in chapter 2). After a short rest perform another jump from a 30-centimeter box and try to reach the same height as the vertical jump test. Continue jumping from progressively higher boxes using 15-centimeter increments until you can no longer reach the original test height. The highest height you can jump from and still reach your test height is the maximum height you should jump from. If you can't attain your test jump height from a 30-centimeter box, you don't have enough strength to do depth jumps and should focus on strength training and lower-intensity plyometrics.

Single-response throws can be done from standing, sitting, or lying positions. They involve a single throw of a medicine ball or weighted object for maximum height or distance. Throws are often combined with jumps into a combined movement.

Multiple-Response Drills

Multiple-response jumps use the skills developed while jumping in place and in standing jumps. The exercises include single- or double-leg jumps for distance over multiple hurdles or objects, or back and forth over a single object. Multiple-response jumps often include changes of direction or body orientation.

Bounds are multiple jumps for maximum distance. Bounds can be done by alternating legs in an exaggerated sprinting stride or with both legs scissoring rapidly.

Hops are normally done over several cones or over and back across an object. The objective of these exercises is to jump as many times as possible in a given time period. Athletes can take off and land on the same leg or both legs simultaneously.

Multiple throws involve throwing a ball back and forth to a partner, catching and releasing the ball as quickly as possible. The goal is to complete a certain number of throws as quickly as possible or complete as many throws as possible in a given period of time.

DESIGNING A PLYOMETRIC PROGRAM

Plyometrics is an intense form of training, which means it can quickly lead to overtraining and overuse injuries. Properly manipulating volume, total number of repetitions, and intensity decreases the risks.

Training intensity   Intensity is a measure of how hard you work and is often compared to the maximum amount of something that you can do. It is a factor in defining the overall stress a training session creates. All repetitions in a plyometric exercise are performed at maximal speed and power. Anything less decreases the stretch-shortening response and plyometric effect of the movement, and therefore reduces the training effect.

The drills and exercises you select will determine the overall intensity of the workout. Table 7.1 ranks the relative intensity for each type of plyometric drill from low to high intensity. Although there are several hundred plyometric movements, this classification system will help you determine which exercises you should do. It will also help you create your own sport-specific exercises. The intensity level of these exercises is determined by the initial prestretch or countermovement prior to the actual movement. Intensity is also determined by the degree of difficulty in performing the movement and the landing. Lunges are classified as low intensity because there is little countermovement or prestretch, and the landing is light. Jumping off a box, landing, then rapidly jumping again is considered high intensity. Whether you land on one leg or two, the intensity level is determined by the initial movement. For example, taking off from one leg is considered a higher intensity movement than taking off from two.

Table 7.1 Relative Intensity of Various Plyometric Drills and Exercises

Drill type	Intensity	Example
Hops	Low	Lateral rope hop, calf hop
Double-limb, single-response jumps and throws	Low-moderate	Vertical jump, standing long jump, box jump, pike jump, tuck jump, overhead toss, med ball chest pass
Full-body, single-response throws	Moderate	Med ball vertical jump and toss, med ball backward toss, med ball long jump and toss, shot put, rotational throw
Double-limb, multiple-response jumps and throws	Moderate-high	Multiple long jumps, repeated vertical jumps, box jump and leap, speed box jump, rope jump
Single-limb, single-response jumps and throws	High	Single-leg vertical jump, single-leg long jump, one-arm chest pass
Single-limb, multiple-response jumps and throws	Very high	Repeated single-leg long jumps, single-leg pattern hop

When progressing through the exercises it is important to understand what constitutes a progressive step. Because you perform plyometrics at maximal speed and power, you can't increase intensity by increasing speed. Therefore, to progress from moderate to high intensity, for example, you could increase the height of the box, which increases the prestretch. Or you could increase the length of a jump or the distance and duration of an exercise. There are too many exercises to discuss every single movement here, but remember this guideline: In general, the higher and longer the distance you cover in an exercise and the faster you perform the movement, the higher the intensity level.

Contacts per session Plyometrics are recorded by the number of single-foot contacts with the ground. For example, 80 contacts are achieved through four sets of 10 reps of a movement that uses both legs, or a total of 80 steps with walking lunges. The volumes listed in table 7.2 represent the total number of contacts per training session, not the number of contacts per exercise. This table assumes that you perform each movement at 100-percent effort. Anything less will not provide the benefit of rapid elastic force production. One exception is when learning a new drill. Perform new drills at 70 to 80 percent until you are comfortable and confident with the technique.

Table 7.2   Plyometric Contacts Per Session

Level	Low intensity	Medium intensity	High intensity
Beginner	80	60	40
Intermediate	100	80	60
Advanced	140	120	100

The numbers in this table represent the number of contacts both feet make with the ground during each training session.

Do not perform plyometrics more than twice a week unless your sport requires movements that accelerate or change direction rapidly. Otherwise two sessions per week is adequate.

Contacts per set Plyometrics is prescribed using sets and reps, just like in strength training. Each plyometric exercise should be done as explosively as possible to develop maximum power. However, your ability to generate speed and power is related to how much energy you have available. The energy for plyometrics comes from the anaerobic (ATP-CP) energy system. These two compounds, adenosine triphosphate and creatine phosphate, known as phosphagens, are available for immediate use. Because the phosphagen stores are relatively small, they can provide energy for only about 5 to 15 seconds of all-out effort. Even though it is possible to keep going once this energy system is significantly reduced, power production will drop to the point that the plyometric exercise is no longer effective for power training. Sets for plyometric box training are normally kept to fewer than six repetitions, unless the rest period between jumps is long. Phosphagen stores will increase with maximal effort training in both strength training exercises and plyometric work. Over time, you will be able to increase your rep number or set time before fatigue sets in (however, it should only increase a rep or two). More likely, you will increase maximal power on each rep, still reducing phosphagen stores.

Rest between sets Rest and recovery are crucial variables in a plyometric program. *Rest* refers to the time between each exercise or set. *Recovery* refers to the amount of time needed before the workout can be repeated.

How much rest you should take depends on the duration of work and the type of drill or exercise you're doing. A rest period can last up to seven minutes between sets or exercises. Table 7.3 offers a guideline for determining rest periods based on how long the exercises take. The work period refers to the time it takes to perform the action and does not necessarily represent the total time to complete each set. For example, when performing a single-response drill you usually take 5 to 10 seconds between reps to reset your body position, which can make the total time for the set a minute or more even though the work time is very short, usually less than one second. Note: Rest for prolonged sets should be between 3 to 5 minutes with between-exercise rest to as much as 10 minutes. Although the fatigue will set in with about 15 seconds, well-conditioned athletes may continue the set for as long as 30 seconds. Realize, however, that longer duration sets begin to reduce the overall effectiveness of maximal power and begin to favor the power conditioning effect (discussed in chapter 8).

Table 7.3 Work and Rest Periods

Work time	Rest between reps (sec)	Rest between sets (min)	Rest between exercises (min)
< 1	5–10	1–2	None
1–3	None	2–3	None
4–15	None	2–4	None
15–30	None	3–5	5–10

Rest periods between sets should last at least two minutes unless the work period is very short. Although popular magazines recommend 30- to 60-second rest periods, shorter periods are not sufficient for the ATP-CP energy system to replenish phosphagen stores or for lactic acid removal. You mainly use the ATP-CP energy system when performing plyometric drills in sets of less than eight repetitions. Once the stored energy is significantly reduced, the body requires about three minutes to fully replace the phosphagens. If you start the next set before the phosphagens are fully restored, the muscles switch to the anaerobic lactic energy system. This results in lactic acid buildup. Therefore, insufficient rest periods decrease the effectiveness of the training program.

Lactic acid is responsible for the burning sensation you experience in the muscles during a difficult or long workout. It also causes feelings of heaviness and fatigue. Some proponents of the "no pain, no gain" theory of exercise mistakenly believe that building up lactic acid promotes increases in muscle size, strength, or power. However, a buildup of lactic acid decreases the quantity and quality of work you're able to perform, which inhibits power gains.

Lactic acid, as noted in chapter 3, is an end product of anaerobic glycolysis, and can decrease the pH in muscle. The enzymes responsible for energy production are very sensitive to changes in pH. Therefore, when the pH drops, these enzymes stop functioning and the muscle fibers are no longer able to produce energy. This means the muscle fiber is no longer capable of participating in the exercise. When enough muscle fibers drop out of the exercise, you're no longer able to perform the exercise. Using an alactic training system (multiple sets of exercise, lasting no more than 10 seconds per set to avoid lactic acid buildup) can decrease the chance of muscle fiber dropout. Another reason to avoid lactic acid buildup is that it interferes with the release and uptake of calcium in the muscle, which is necessary for muscle contraction.

If rest between sets is insufficient, lactic acid will accumulate not only in the muscle but also in the blood. Once in the blood, lactic acid is transported to all parts of the body and negatively affects the performance of other muscles, too. Therefore, training one muscle group to failure decreases the quantity and quality of work done by another muscle group.

Lactic acid buildup also can increase your chance of injury. When muscle fibers start to drop out of an exercise, technique gets sloppy. Muscle fiber dropout also makes it more difficult to establish motor patterns. It is more difficult to learn a new exercise when you are producing high levels of lactic acid.

Although shorter rest periods might make you think you are working harder, in the long run you will defeat the purpose of plyometric training. Fatigue will keep you from performing the exercises explosively, thereby reducing your ability to develop power. For conditioning and power development while fatigued, shorter rest periods are recommended. Realize however, that while fatigued, your maximal power development will not improve, only your power while fatigued. This may be especially effective as you begin to near the season in sports such as basketball where explosive jumping is mixed with sprints and activity that lasts more than 15 seconds.

BODY-WEIGHT PLYOMETRIC DRILLS

Before progressing to complex and demanding drills that require jumping onto or over obstacles, it is best to perfect technique using body-weight plyometric drills. In fact, body-weight drills may be all that you need to sufficiently develop the stretch-shortening cycle, especially for athletes that are only using plyometrics sparingly in their training. Additionally, to increase the difficulty of a body-weight drill, try doing them on one leg! One-leg drills are great for the "single-support" (meaning standing on one leg) situations you may encounter in your particular sport, especially when you are in an off-balance position. Body-weight plyometrics are great for soccer players and athletes that are involved in sports that are more aerobic in nature than anaerobic. These will help develop power at a level that is more appropriate for the endurance athlete. Keep in mind that body-weight plyometrics may be performed when you are fatigued to add an overload effect that may be more specific to the endurance sport athlete (the person who needs to be able to jump or react at the end of the game, such as heading a soccer ball). Remember, if you perform plyometric drills while fatigued, the net effect of the power training will be reduced when trying to develop single maximal effort power.

Vertical (or Squat) Jump

Stand with the feet about shoulder-width apart. Swing the arms back and quickly dip until the knees bend to about 120 degrees (*a*). Explode upward extending the knees, hips, ankles, and trunk while swinging the arms forward and upward as explosively as possible. Focus on completely extending the body, reaching as high as possible. The arm drive is critical for achieving maximum jump height.

For a variation, commonly referred to as the tuck jump, pull the knees into the chest (*b*), grabbing them with both hands before landing (*c*).

a   *b*   *c*

Lateral Jump

Stand with the feet shoulder-width apart. Swing the arms back and quickly dip until the knees bend to about 120 degrees (*a*). Explode laterally extending the knees, hips, ankles, and trunk while swinging the arms forward and laterally as explosively as possible (*b*) before landing (*c*).

a   *b*   *c*

Split Jump

Begin in a proper lunge position with the forward leg flat on the ground and the back leg on the toes. The front leg should be bent at 90 degrees. The trunk should be upright (a). The body should remain in this position throughout the drill. Thrust the arms upward and extend the legs so that the body moves explosively upward (b). The athlete should switch his legs quickly in the air so that when he lands, he is in the opposite leg position than that which he started in (c).

a

b

c

Speed Skater

Begin in the same position as the lateral jump. Cock the arms over to the right side (a). Explosively extend the knee, hip, ankle, and trunk while simultaneously thrusting the arms to the left side (b). Laterally jump from the left leg to the right leg (c). Land on the right leg, dropping into the same position that the drill began in, and then repeat the action back and forth.

a

b

c

Plyometric Push-Up

Begin in a push-up position (*a*). If the athlete is not strong enough to do a regular push-up, the modified "knees on the ground" position may be assumed. This drill is performed like a push-up; however, as the athlete comes up, extending the arms, he will do it explosively, trying to leave the ground. Often coaches will have the athlete attempt to clap his hands in the air (*b*) so that the he generates enough power and "air time" to effectively complete this drill and return to the starting position (*c*). This is a difficult exercise for athletes that have insufficient upper-body strength.

a

b

c

HURDLE DRILLS

Hurdles are used to develop many skills within athletes. Hopping drills are certainly classified as plyometric in nature and provide a stimulus that helps an athlete jump higher, farther, and quicker. Each of the drills that are done with hurdles can be performed for either speed or height. Speed hopping drills work on decreasing amortization time, helping explosive leg turnover, while height or distance jump drills work on both explosive strength in the hip extensors and hip flexors. When jumping, if you rapidly pull your legs to you (as in the vertical jump) you will improve hip flexor speed and thus improve leg turnover speed. In either case (pulling your knees to your chest or not) explosive height or distance jumps improve hip extensor power. These drills should emphasize power and should be short in nature so ideally six hurdles will be sufficient. When designing these drills, be specific as to whether you are looking to develop vertical height (ideal for basketball and volleyball) or horizontal speed with limited height (football, tennis, soccer). When jumping the athlete should be able to "stick" the landing and maintain proper body position even when moving rapidly across the hurdles. Do not let momentum carry you through the drill so that you are literally falling at the end. All drills can be performed with one leg or two.

Linear Hurdle Hop for Height

Set up the hurdles in a straight line. Hop over the hurdles, jumping as high as possible, taking off and landing on two feet. Focus on maximizing height and pulling the knees up during the jump (*a*, *b*, and *c*).

a

b

c

An option for this drill is to complete lateral hurdle hops for height. Set up the hurdles in a straight line. Hop over the hurdles sideways, jumping as high as possible and taking off and landing on two feet. Focus on maximizing height and pulling the knees up during the jump.

Linear Hurdle Hop for Speed

Set up the hurdles in a straight line. Hop over the hurdles as quickly as possible, taking off and landing on two feet (*a* and *b*). Focus on minimizing the ground time between jumps.

An option for this drill is to complete lateral hurdle hops for speed. Set up the hurdles in a straight line. Hop over the hurdles sideways as quickly as possible, taking off and landing on two feet. Focus on minimizing the ground time between jumps.

a

b

Single-Leg Linear Hurdle Hop for Speed

Perform this drill the same as the linear hurdle hop for speed, but hop on one leg (*a*, *b*, and *c*). After completing the drill on one leg, repeat it on the other.

An option is to perform this drill the same as the lateral hurdle hop for speed, but hop on one leg. After completing the drill on one leg, repeat it on the other leg.

a

b

c

Hurdles Backward

Place a series of hurdles two feet from each other in a straight line. Stand with your back to the hurdles and jump backward over each one by extending the ankles and driving the knees and hips up (*a*, *b*, and *c*). Explosively swing the arms upward. Focus on decreasing the time on the ground between hurdles. Keep your weight balanced over the front of the feet, waist slightly bent, shoulders facing forward, and head up. Land on the balls of the feet, with knees bent.

a

b

c

Hurdles Diagonal

Place a series of hurdles in a zig-zag pattern. Place the first hurdle and the next one at a 90-degree angle to the following one. Following this pattern, place the remaining hurdles (six to eight hurdles total). Begin by jumping forward extending the knees, hips, and ankles (*a* and *b*). Immediately upon landing (*c*), jump over the next hurdle. Then repeat this process for the remaining hurdles. Focus on decreasing the time on the ground between hurdles. Keep your weight balanced over the front of the feet, waist slightly bent, shoulders facing forward, and head up. Land on the balls of the feet, with knees bent.

a

b

c

Hurdles 90 Degrees

Place a series of hurdles two feet from each other in a straight line. Jump forward over the first hurdle (a), and while in midair make a half turn to the left (b and c). On the next jump, make a half turn back to the center. Over the third hurdle make a half turn toward the right. The next jump will be a half turn back to the center. Repeat this process over the series of hurdles.

a   b   c

MEDICINE BALL TRAINING

Training with weighted objects dates back to the early 1900s; however, more recently, the use of medicine balls to increase strength and conditioning has gained popularity. This type of training provides several advantages, and despite its disadvantages, it can add variety to stale training routines. Medicine balls come in a variety of shapes, sizes, and weights. In fact, now medicine balls are being made with handles and ropes for gripping while doing activities such as rotational throws. Choosing ball weight and size is based on training goals (see chapter 11 for some suggested routines). For more speed, the ball should be smaller and lighter, while a heavier ball tends to become more strength-speed or even power. As an athlete becomes stronger, the ball will move faster and thus the progression to the next size is necessary.

The medicine ball, also known as a med ball, is a versatile training tool. It can serve many purposes, depending on how it is used in a conditioning program. Med balls can help develop flexibility, muscular endurance, and power. Although many advocates believe that med ball training that mimics a sports movement directly transfers to sports improvement, I do not. Studies and literature supporting these benefits are minimal, and consist mainly of claims made by medicine ball manufacturers and sellers, and authors of med ball training programs. Med ball training is an effective way to build explosive power as well as muscular endurance through a circuit.

The med ball can be used to develop speed by using very light-weight balls traveling very fast or for power by using heavier balls with explosive movements. As a speed training tool it is best used for rotational and other movement activities where the ball is not released. The emphasis should be on quick direction changes. As a power training tool, a med ball is best used with strong release efforts using rotational movements or pressing and pushing-like activities.

When learning a new exercise, the first physiological adaptations are neurological improvements in fiber recruitment and general coordination. To build pure strength, medicine balls are not heavy enough for most athletes to produce an overload inside the five- to eight-rep range. For power, on the other hand, medicine balls present a very realistic challenge. As we saw on the force–velocity curve and in the definition of power, rapidly moving a low weight generates more power than moving a heavier weight more slowly. To improve endurance through med ball training, decrease the rest between sets and exercises, or increase the number of reps, or both.

Medicine ball training, when done correctly, is a safe form of resistance training. However, the incidence of injury can be high if you do not perform the exercises properly. You should learn proper technique by progressing sensibly from lighter to heavier balls and practicing exercises in a slow, nonballistic fashion that is controlled rather than explosive. Do not perform single-arm overhead throws (like a football throw). Although some believe this type of motion provides benefits, the risk of injury outweighs the benefits. And if you believe in the theory of specificity, then skill transfer is impossible, because balancing a large, oddly shaped object while cocking the arm back is hardly similar to throwing a baseball or football. In fact, this activity may actually impair your regular throwing motion, causing you to compensate, or teach you a completely different (but specific to medicine balls) skill. Another reason to avoid single-arm throws is that the risk of shoulder injury is much greater than in double-arm movements. However, medicine ball training, like any explosive exercise, can reap great benefit with minimal risk if properly supervised.

You can perform medicine ball training alone or with a partner. If alone, use a brick wall as a target for most exercises. The wall or partner should be at least 20 feet away. Unless an exercise calls for directly catching the ball, let it bounce before catching it. Many avoidable injuries happen when an athlete reaches for the ball with a one-handed grab.

Start Positions

Medicine ball exercises start in one of four basic positions. The athlete can lie face up (supine), sit, kneel, or stand. Each position requires a different type of throw, which provides four possibilities for most exercises. Standing is the most common position for most athletes and sports. When standing, the lower body generates the power for the movement. Kneeling is the least common and places stress on the knees. The supine position starts most sit-up and abdominal exercises and can be modified by adding a bend in the knees. Sitting isolates the upper body and prevents the legs from helping with the production of force.

Basic Throws

There are four types of throws, with several offshoots. The overhead throw is similar to a soccer throw-in. The push throw is most similar to a chest pass or bench press pass. The underhand throw starts between the legs or below the waist. A throw originating from the side involves a twisting motion. Each type of throw can be adapted. A general med ball program uses each of the four throws. An exercise using a side throw should be done on both sides, the same number of reps on each side.

By combining the four throws and the four starting positions, you can create at least 16 different throws. The total number of exercises is limited only by your creativity in combining exercises. Like in all athletic training, proper technique is paramount. If the goal is to move the med ball explosively, then move it explosively.

Two-Hand Twist Toss

Stand sideways, holding the med ball like a batter would hold a bat, with the knees slightly bent and the waist slightly bent (a). Next, pull back and fire, with both arms being kept straight while moving with the hips and legs to rotate (b) (the other version is completely bent over at the waist). Keeping the arms straight, throw the ball as far as possible (c). The pivot on the toes and driving the hips around, not the waist rotation, generates the power for this throw.

a

b

c

V-Up

Lie on your back with the legs straight and the hands extended overhead holding the med ball (*a*). Simultaneously raise your legs and trunk into a seated V position, keeping the ball overhead (*b*). Hold this position for a two count (*c*). Return to the starting position, performing another rep as soon as the trunk and legs touch the ground. Perform this drill slowly until you establish your balance point. Once established, use quicker and more explosive movements.

a

b

c

Seated Trunk Rotation

Sit in a V-up position, holding the med ball with both hands at arms length in front of the chest (*a*). Keeping the arms straight, rotate from the trunk, turning as far as you can while maintaining the V-up position (*b*). Quickly rotate back to the other side. Keep the ball at chest height, moving only from the waist, following the ball with the head and shoulders.

a

b

Sit-Up Toss

Lie on your back with knees bent and feet flat. Raise the torso off the ground. When you are at the top of the sit-up position, raise the hands over the head. A partner will toss you a med ball. Catch it and allow the weight to take you back to the starting position (*a*). As soon as the shoulder blades touch the ground, explode upward and toss the ball back to your partner (*b*). The abdominal muscles should generate most of the power for the throw with the arms coming into play only for the final toss. The partner standing must accurately throw the ball into your hands so you can establish a rhythm. Curl rather than jerk the torso off the ground to ensure that you use the abdominals' entire range of motion. If you perform the drill with the feet free, the abdominal muscles do most of the work. If someone or something holds the feet, the hip flexors do most of the work.

a

b

Twisting Sit-Up Toss

Lie on your back with knees bent and feet flat. Raise the torso off the ground (*a*). When you are at the top of the sit-up position, raise the hands over the head. A partner will toss the med ball over your head to one side of your body (*b*). Rotate the trunk to catch the ball, and allow the weight to take you back to the ground; however, in this exercise keep the trunk twisted as you lower it. As soon as the shoulder blade touches the ground sit up, maintaining the twist and throw the ball back to your partner. The abdominal muscles should generate most of the power for the throw with the arms coming into play only for the final toss. The partner standing must accurately throw the ball so you can establish a rhythm. Curl rather than jerk the torso off the ground to ensure that you use the abdominals' entire range of motion. If you perform the drill with the feet free, the abdominal muscles do most of the work. If someone or something holds the feet, the hip flexors do most of the work.

a

b

Lying Power Drop

You need a partner and a box, bench, or chair (drop height of five to six feet) for this drill. Lie on your back with the head near the box, knees bent, feet flat, arms extended straight over the chest, and the hands in position to catch the ball. Your partner stands on the bench holding the ball directly over your hands then drops the ball (*a*). Catch the ball and absorb the impact as quickly as possible so you can throw the ball back up to the person on the box (*b*). Both partners must throw accurately so that they can establish a rhythm. You can also do this drill with two balls and three people. The third person catches the throw from the person on the ground and hands the ball to the person on the box. As everyone becomes comfortable with the drill, the person on the box can throw the ball down rather than dropping it, increasing the force that must be absorbed and the prestretch.

a

b

Two-Hand Overhead Throw

Hold the med ball over the head in both hands. Feet are shoulder-width apart. Bend the elbows to lower the ball behind the head (*a*), then step forward and throw the ball as far as possible (*b*).

a

b

Axe Chop

Hold a medicine ball with both hands (*a*) over one shoulder and twist the upper body toward that side (*b*). Using the lower body to generate power, snap the hips and torso toward the other side and aggressively drive the ball diagonally downward across the body (*c*). Release the ball directly into the ground.

a   *b*   *c*

Ancient Log Throw

Begin in a squat position holding a grip ball in one hand or medicine ball in both hands between the legs (a). In one quick movement, bring the arms upward (b) and over the head. Release the ball when the hands are at chest level and follow through (c). In order for this drill to be effective, it must be performed in one explosive movement. Note: This drill can be done with one arm or both arms.

a

b

c

LOWER-BODY POWER DRILLS

Lower-body drills are designed around body-weight activities and improve power in jumping-related sports such as basketball and volleyball. Additionally, the power developed here helps overall hip power that will help most other athletes. To provide additional stimulus, add weight or combine movement activities. When using a box for plyometrics, select a height between 12 and 24 inches. While very skilled athletes can use boxes as high as 36 inches, for most athletes, 12 to 18 inches is best. Remember, when jumping, if your recovery from the jump takes too long, the value of the drill is lost. If you use a high box to jump to, use quick hip flexion to get the legs up, then step down rather than jump. These drills can be modified to include resistive tubing and med balls. Body-weight plyometrics are best for athletes that fall into the speed-strength or explosive power categories, whereas additional weighted plyometrics are best for explosive power and strength-speed athletes.

Jump Up Onto Box

Stand next to a box and begin this drill like the squat jump (a). Squat down using proper squat technique (see page 156). Once you've reached the bottom of the squat, explode into the air fully extending the arms (b) and land on the box (c). For an extra challenge you may use a medicine ball. Hold the ball at chest height with both hands and extend the arms during the movement.

a

b

c

For a variation, take this drill one step further by completing the following steps. Begin by standing on top of the box (you may hold a med ball at chest height). Step off the box and upon impact, immediately jump back up. The initial drop from the box maximizes the plyometric effect by increasing the prestretch. It also increases the amount of force you must overcome when jumping back onto the box.

Depth Jumps

To really enhance the difficulty of a jump, a depth jump or depth jump series may be used. Depth jumps are very demanding and should only be performed by well-conditioned athletes and/or those weighing less than 240 pounds (108.86 kilograms). The athlete steps off a high box (*a*) (usually 24 to 36 inches) and immediately upon ground contact, absorbs the landing (*b*) and begins to jump back up (*c*). You should try to minimize ground contact time and you can increase the difficulty by jumping off the box rather than stepping off.

a

b

c

Note: There are several different box jump exercises. If you have multiple boxes, you can line them up in series and jump from box to box in a similar fashion to the previous exercises (*a*, *b*, and *c*).

a

b

c

COMPLEX TRAINING

Complexes are a series of exercises done in quick succession. They can be used to improve conditioning or build explosive power. Dumbbell and body-weight complexes use relatively light weights and fit into the speed–strength continuum somewhere between strength-speed and power. To build power, explosively perform two or three reps of each exercise. To improve conditioning, do six to eight reps of each exercise. Move quickly from one exercise to the next using the same set of dumbbells for the entire complex. Create your own complexes to simulate your sport needs and your desired training effect. The following complexes will get you started.

Dumbbell Complex 1

Upright row
High-pull snatch
Squat push press
Bent-over row
Power snatch

Dumbbell Complex 2

Upright row
High-pull snatch
Squat and press
Good morning
Bent-over row

Dumbbell Complex 3

Biceps curl
Upright row
Bent-over row
High-pull snatch
Shoulder press
Squat push press

Plyometric-Dumbbell Complex

Squats
Vertical jumps
Split-lunge jumps
Split jerk
Clean to press

You've learned how to increase your speed and strength and combine them to produce powerful movements in a workout. The next chapter explains how these movements become second nature so you can produce them during competition.

8

Transferring Training to Performance

Although speed and strength are important, the strongest, fastest athlete does not always win or dominate a sport. We have seen several athletes, successful in one sport, try to master another and fail. We have also seen lifters and sprinters try to play team sports with little success. Why doesn't their speed and strength carry over? Because the skills and movements necessary to excel in a particular sport are specific to that sport, and these athletes have spent years teaching their bodies and muscles to produce those movements. In most team sports, opponents are blocking your progress. Being able to sprint 100 meters in a straight line does not mean you will be able to break away or laterally move around an opponent with success. To further complicate matters, having the skill to catch, kick, or pass while in movement are skills that take years to master.

Once you have improved your speed and strength and combined them to produce power, you have the ingredients for sports success. Now comes the tricky part: making what you have achieved in training work for you in competition.

REPS, LOTS OF THEM

The name of the game is reps. Coaches say, "We need more reps," meaning that you need to practice the timing, execution, and technique to produce the desired effect. More important, because everyone is different, responds differently to training, and has his or her own mental approach to sport, the timing between athletes of team sports is especially crucial. Research shows that it takes between 5,000 and 15,000 repetitions to master a skill. Although that may seem easily achievable, keep in mind that those reps must be perfect; otherwise you're simply practicing and reinforcing bad habits. This need for more reps explains why so many recreational golfers struggle with their golf game. Twenty rounds of golf per year will not provide enough reps. Thus, for power training to be useful, both the skills for your sport and techniques for power training must be practiced concurrently and with enough reps to achieve a transfer of training effect onto the field. And although your sport-specific skills such as shooting, hitting, throwing, and so forth are vital to the outcome of the game, it is necessary to incorporate your power development into the training program for a useable training modality. Chapters 9 and 11 show you how to put your program together. But first we need to learn how the body adapts and what we need to do to help it.

© Empics

Keeping your eyes on your opponent and dribbling a basketball are two skills that require a lot of practice (or reps) to fully master.

To understand how difficult training sport-specific movements is, consider this: Even a simple task must be perfected before the muscles can work together efficiently. For example, electromyography shows that when curling a weight, the two heads of the biceps do not work together until training has been perfected through weeks of training.

This example shows that even two heads of the same muscle must learn to work together. Now imagine a more complex movement requiring almost every joint and their corresponding

EMG

Electromyography (EMG) is a method of determining and identifying the contribution of individual muscle activity during a particular movement. It is done using either surface or in-muscle electrodes that monitor the electrical activity of motor units. Recall that during recruitment, motor units are called in to do a specific task and the more force or precision needed, the more motor units (or more specific motor units) are called into play. The EMG picks up this information allowing us to visually see muscle contribution. However, EMG has its limitations in that muscle activity and actual force production are not perfectly related (due to biomechanical factors described in chapter 3 among other reasons). Smoothing EMG refers to the process during the analysis that takes out other bodily electrical activity (such as heart beat and other "noise" from other muscles). When EMG patterns are erratic, muscles are not firing in synch. With even just a few weeks of training (two to four), muscles begin to synchronize, suggesting that a more refined recruitment pattern is developing (see figures 8.1, *a* and *b*).

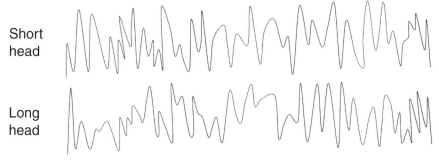

FIGURE 8.1a *Smoothed EMG curves show how the short and long heads of the biceps brachii do not work together.*

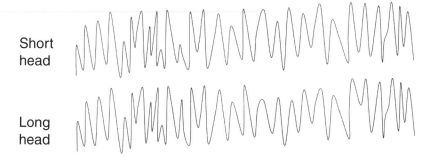

FIGURE 8.1b *Smoothed EMG curves show how the short and long heads of the biceps brachii are synchronized after weeks of training.*

muscles. For example, in walking, more than 50 pairs (each side of the body) of muscles are involved in the lower body, and this does not include the muscles that swing the arms, or keep the torso and head upright. Although easy for you now, walking wasn't always. No one remembers the complicated and time-intensive process of learning how to walk, but in a nutshell, it comes down to reps. You repeat thousands of actions every single day for a year or more. During this learning process there is a progression, where several thousand reps will occur as well. Since the process of walking (when you are a child especially) requires balance, coordination, and strength, each progression the child makes from holding his head up, to sitting up, to crawling, and then standing requires specific muscle activation patterns (known as neuromuscular education or motor learning). The mistakes made (such as falling over) are then discarded and a new pattern of activation is attempted. This process continues until the skill is mastered. Interestingly though, we continue to learn our entire life and as our body changes, so too do our recruitment patterns. This is how we are able to balance as we age and the effects of overeating, osteoporosis, and poor posture begin to take over.

Now imagine the difficult task of synchronizing muscles to perform complex movements such as throwing at high velocity using the entire body. You see why it can take years to perfect. Every time a muscle contracts to produce movement, other muscles relax or stabilize. Continuing that same movement, the muscles that were just contracting relax and let other muscles take over. Recall in muscle function, if you contract antagonistic muscles at the same time you will not be able to move (meaning that if I want to contract both my biceps and triceps, my arm would not move at the elbow). Therefore, timing is essential, and it occurs within 10ths or even 100ths of a second. Scientists have tried to study the constant on–off stabilization of muscles for decades. The complexity of a single movement coupled with some of the things humans do astounds biomechanists. Examples of this include a pitcher throwing a 100 mile-per-hour ball into a one foot by one foot box (the strike zone), or a gymnast coming off the rings or uneven bars in the dismount doing a double twisting flip and sticking the landing (not to mention the disorienting effects alone take "recovery" to spot the landing).

What does this mean for power development in particular and training in general? Your body's ability to perform movement depends on storing and retrieving neural data in a complex filing system. You can modify the data through the actions you practice in training. Using power training to update the data in your "filing system" can improve athletic performance.

FROM THOUGHT TO EXECUTION

The human brain is like a giant sponge. It continually collects millions of bits of information and stores them in a unique filing system. Each time you perform an action, the instructions for performing the action are permanently etched in your brain. But rather than organizing information chronologically or alphabetically, the brain stores data based on how often you retrieve it. Therefore, the more you practice, the more accessible is the data and the better you get at retrieving it, which allows you to perform the skill faster and more efficiently. The opposite is also true; if you don't retrieve the neural data frequently, performance suffers. The good news is that the brain never throws anything away; it just stores it a little deeper for later use. That's why if you haven't ridden a bike in years, you could probably hop on one, and after a shaky start, take a spin around the block. The following discussion offers more tips to ingrain movement sequences and power into your "filing system."

Building the perfect filing system The more you train each specific component of your skill set and the more you practice the entire skill, the better you become at it. In the case of developing explosive power, you must work on speed and strength, then combine the two through practice. Cut right, dodge a punch, jump to block the shot—all these sports movements require power. Why do some athletes perform them better, more quickly, and with more grace? Some athletes use their filing systems more effectively. They have amassed thousands of reps to build the perfect filing system—a system that calls upon specific muscles in a specific sequence as quickly as possible. Developing the optimal pathway to call upon speed and strength is the key to developing optimal power.

Processing center The brain is frequently compared to a computer's microprocessor. Producing different movement requires different levels of processing. Reflexive actions—pulling your hand away from a hot stove—don't have to be learned, and they happen quickly. Unfortunately, patterned human movements, like those used in sport, are not processed so quickly. This is why the filing system is important. Various structures within the brain are responsible for examining and controlling balance, coordination, and the force of contraction (magnitude of force developed). When a signal, or request for a particular movement, enters the brain, it is rate coded, graded, and sent to the motor cortex to initiate movement. Rate coding is the process of identifying what the stimulus is and examining the type of stimulus by determining frequency, magnitude, and position. Grading is then deciding what the response action will be, according to the rate coded information. The combination of continual rate coding and grading refines the signal that will be countered by a movement pattern. The more complex the intended movement, the longer it takes to rate code it. Vision, hearing, and other senses help to rate code the requested movement. Training your system to recognize and interpret information through practice and reps improves your ability to move. Because power is the rate of performing work, the faster you can send signals through the brain network, the more power you can create. Just like a faster CPU speeds up your computer, a faster pathway for neural signals speeds up athletic performance.

Motor cortex When a signal has been refined, a specific program is sent to the motor cortex to initiate the movement sequence. The faster the information gets to the motor cortex, the faster you can execute a movement. The pattern is maintained via feedback mechanisms that send information back and forth through your filing system to refine the skill. Feedback may be both positive and negative. With positive feedback, the suggested response continues through the filing system adding balance, coordination, and grading the force. With negative feedback, the filing system sends a new message to be cleared for processing. Unfortunately, in explosive movements, negative feedback tends to be too late, and you usually are unable to perform the skill properly (such as reacting too soon, or overreacting). The negative feedback system is how we learn to do a skill, the positive feedback mechanism makes the skill more precise. Fortunately, the brain is rather plastic in nature, and can be reshaped so that more nerve tissue is available in areas where more motor activity is required. And more motor activity is required in areas that require more precise movement.

Training refines the filing system by forcing the nerve tissue to "rewire" the signal process to be more efficient. In the case of producing more strength, training rewires the system to call more muscle fibers into the activity. This process is known as recruitment. Superior athletes possess a superior ability to recruit muscle fibers to perform a task with speed, strength, or power. When you first perform a new movement, it takes time to perfect it (riding a bicycle for the first time). As you practice, your brain refines your skills, engrains the specific motor pattern, and recruits the correct muscle fibers in the optimal sequence to perform a coordinated movement. Developing power then is a matter of speeding up this sequence and calling up more muscle fibers to perform the task. Thus powerful athletes are trained, not born.

Develop a training program that speeds the processing time and you will develop into a more powerful athlete. That seems simple enough. But, it's not that simple. You must also take into consideration the rules for particular sports, coordination of teammates playing various positions, and willingness of an athlete to continue, even when he is exhausted.

Perfecting movement Recall from our discussion in chapter 7 that plyometric and explosive activities require that you execute movements at 100 percent effort level, and that even a small drop in effort hampers results. The key to building explosive power that you can transfer to sport is to train movements just as they are required in sport. The rule of specificity says that for specific adaptation to take effect, you must place a specific stress on the appropriate system. Therefore, select speed and strength drills that mimic movements in your sport, and design a training program of sets, reps, and rest that reflects your sport's requirements. But be careful! Training sport-like movements alone will not directly transfer to your game. Moving an object different from what you use in competition and following a pattern different from your sports movement produces only a minimal carryover effect. Although practicing with a weighted implement, for example swinging an overweight tennis racket, provides benefits, too much of this type of training can hinder performance. You run the risk of adjusting your swing to accommodate the heavier implement, which may throw off your timing when using your normal equipment.

The more specific and sport-like your strength training, the more you must integrate it into your skill training. For example, if you're a shot putter, working bench presses to develop upper-body strength will not interfere with your throwing technique. The body will not confuse the motion of the bench press with the pushing motion to propel the shot. However, explosive, one-arm, alternating incline presses with a dumbbell could cause the body to try to adapt differently. Therefore, to reduce the chance of a negative carryover effect, it is important to integrate these dumbbell presses into the program when the athlete is also working on throwing technique.

Transferring training power to performance power As you have seen, the movements used in power training do not directly carry over to power performance. So how do you integrate your plyometric activity, speed work, and strength gains to produce power? How do you increase your strength without producing unwanted training effects? You can do so by designing a program that slowly brings about the change. For optimal gains in power, train for periods of

DEVELOPING POWER TRAINING PROGRAMS UNDER FATIGUE

Training power while fatigued is probably the most demanding form of training. Using a series of explosive exercises coupled with already fast-paced exercises takes willpower and smart planning. Tolerance is the name of the game. You will feel that lactic acid buildup and begin to burn, forcing the easy decision to quit. Quitting is not an option unless losing is something you are willing to accept.

You should develop training routines that use explosive movements for six to eight reps lasting no more than about 10 to 15 seconds. The more demanding the explosive movement, the less reps you should perform. An active rest (such as running) between the explosive sets should be used and should last about 20 to 30 seconds. The cycle of explosive movement–active rest should last about two minutes. Then after a cycle of activity is completed a rest of three to five minutes should be taken. As you get in shape, rest time should be decreased and overall pace should increase.

Typically, the active rest is running and the distances covered should be similar to your sport. A tennis player, for example, may shuffle or sprint back and forth across the court for 20 seconds, then perform explosive split jumps for five or six reps. To make things more difficult you may add backward running to the drill. Commonly, coaches will employ agility drills for the active rest with explosive plyometric jumps to build power while under fatigued situations.

three to five weeks with skill training occurring during and after. Because power workouts require tremendous contributions from the neurological system, you must schedule them to allow optimal recovery, or adaptation, to take place. To avoid delayed-onset muscle soreness (DOMS), schedule 48 to 72 hours between power workouts. I recommend an every-other-day or twice a week per body part type of training routine. Neural damage, the equivalent of DOMS, may take as much as 120 hours for complete recovery. Most people, however, do not take this much recovery because most people fail to train at 100-percent effort. Keep your power training focused and recover properly.

As you approach your season, match your rep and rest time to the sport. Regular plyometric training uses three- to five-minute rest periods to stimulate maximal power development. However, as your season gets closer, shift to fewer reps with maximal effort and shorter rest between sets. Although this goes against the general rules of power training, this change will help you channel your power into sports movements. For sports that require continual power applications mixed within regular sports movements such as sports that sit at the speed-strength and power portion of the continuum such as tennis, football, volleyball, etc., integrate the power movements into the conditioning process. For example, a common conditioning routine for basketball players is *suicides*. In the following drill (figure 8.2), I've added a plyometric component before each sprint.

At position 1, do split jumps, six to eight done with maximal effort (that is important in all of these) then walking lunges to the free-throw line and back. At position 2, do five squat jumps, then sprint to half court and back. At position 3, do five speed skaters, then sprint to the opposite foul line and back. At position 4, do five plyometric push-ups, and sprint to the other end of the court

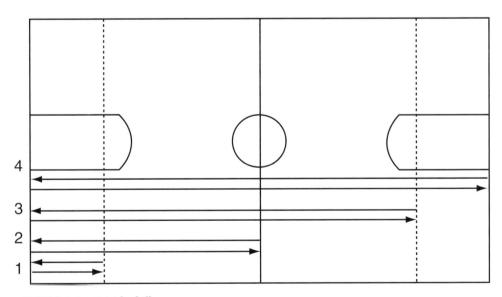

FIGURE 8.2   Suicide drills.

and back. Because this is primarily a conditioning exercise, take no rest between each position. When you return to the end line, take a two-minute rest, then do it again. Follow the second set by a three-minute rest, then do one more set.

This is an example of one of the many ways to incorporate power into the overall training program, while focusing on generating power even when you are fatigued. As you become more fit, this exercise becomes easy, and you should be able to complete this series six times with 30 to 60 seconds between sets.

It's not enough to do it just at game time   Power training is demanding and requires 100-percent effort. Therefore, you must practice hard every day to build the foundation for sports power. Every rep, every set, and every exercise is important. This attitude will pay off late in the game or event. If you've put in the necessary effort during workouts and practices, you won't come up short wishing you had more to offer. Remember, great athletes work hard all of the time, not most or some of the time. This means you must approach a practice or workout as if it were game time every time. Rest means rest. Doing a workout just to do one does not improve your sports power. Understanding why you are doing specific workouts, realizing that maximal effort is necessary, and realizing proper execution is vital for improvement will make your workouts more valuable. If you are trying to condition yourself for power, make sure that you are

The hard work of an athlete, such as a javelin thrower, during workouts and practices can pay off during competition.

pacing yourself properly so that powerful movements can be integrated properly into the endurance-like activity—and remember, power-endurance workouts are extremely demanding.

Now that you understand how the brain develops a filing system to create powerful movements, it's time to develop a program that will transform your reps to sport skill. The next chapter explains how to divide a training program into phases—each with a specific goal—and then how to focus on each phase as you progress through your season.

9

Power Cycles Through Periodization

Athletes and coaches have used the principles of periodization to structure their training for years. Although formalized and popularized in the former East bloc countries, periodized training may have been around for centuries (although the concept wasn't yet known by that name). If you consider it in its simplest form—the training year is split into different periods, each with a specific goal—most athletes use some form of periodization for their training.

Periodization is not the only training method. Several training philosophies state that the athlete should always train maximally and train the same way. The only change within the program is in the exercise selection. If you believe in specificity and overload, then a nonperiodized theory holds water. However, I have to argue that periodization occurs in these programs anyway because the training sessions vary according to the athlete's needs. At different times during the training year he will rest, modify the program, and change the rep scheme, thereby breaking down the training into periods. Therefore, I call these programs the modified periodized method. A periodized training program—either true periodization or the modified method—with planned variety keeps the muscles and the athlete interested in the work that must be done. It also encourages the athlete and the coach to plan goals, reach them, and exceed them with new personal records.

TWO PRINCIPLES OF PERIODIZATION

Hans Selye, a brilliant early-20th-century physician and considered by many to be the reason why periodization came about, suggested that the body undergoes adaptation by responding to stimulus. The stimulus shocks the system, which causes the body to react by supercompensating, or compensating more than necessary. Selye postulated that the body responds to physical stress by adapting, becoming proficient, then eventually becoming stale. To continue to see physical gains, an athlete must continue the process of stimulation and supercompensation. To give the body a new challenge, the athlete needs a new stimulus. But rather than throwing any old activity at her body, it makes sense to train an athletic aspect that she needs. Which leads to the second principle behind periodization: specificity.

Cyclists periodize their training by working on specific elements such as hill climbing and short sprints.

Specificity means that you train the body for a specific adaptation, and that adaptation should be specific to your sport and your goals. Today, specificity is one of the most fundamental approaches to training. When training power, you must be specific in your training program so that you actually improve power and not just increase speed or strength. This chapter helps you understand how to use periodization to improve power.

The periodized training model must be structured. It must consist of specific phases, cycles, sessions, and periods, all set up in advance and each with a specific goal. For example, a high school football player's season goes from August through December. In today's competitive environment, athletes are expected to be in shape at the start of preseason camp, and thus the training program that leads up to August must be specifically designed to prepare an athlete for preseason, two-a-day practices.

Most periodized training programs are planned on a yearly basis. However, they can be shorter than that or longer.

In fact, many world-class athletes plan their training programs around the four years between Olympic Games—peaking for the Olympics. But no matter how long your program is, you must have a training plan. For example, if you're a world-class thrower, your goal for your entire training program might be to set a world record at the Olympics. You will progress toward your ultimate goal by setting and reaching incremental training and competitive goals, such as placing at or winning a national championship.

A periodized plan is broken into many different phases. To fully understand periodization, it's important to learn the terminology for the different phases.

Macrocycle   This is the largest period, encompassing all of the individual periods. It is usually based on a 12-month cycle.

Mesocycle   This is a shorter period within the macrocycle. One mesocycle may last as few as four weeks to as long as three to four months. A mesocycle is usually defined as a particular phase of the sport season; however, in sports with competitions throughout the year, it may be defined as a specific training period.

Microcycle   This is the shortest period defined by general periodization standards. It may last one to four weeks or even one or two workouts. Several microcycles make up a mesocycle.

Nanocycle and picacycle   These are smaller periods within the general phasic cycling program. These may refer to specific days or even specific events within a particular training day.

Preseason   The preseason is usually the longest period within a cycle. It is the period after the postseason layoff. It begins well before the season starts and ends before preseason or regular games or regular practices begin.

In-season   This is the period in which competition or games are staged.

Postseason or off-season   I prefer the term postseason because it usually refers to a period of active rest (unless you're injured), and off-season may imply that you're doing nothing. This period is short compared to the preseason and in-season.

An event   During each cycle are specific workouts. Each workout may be considered a specific event whereby a set of tasks are clearly separated and defined.

Endurance phase   During this phase the athlete spends most of his time working on muscular endurance. This phase is characterized by long sets of many reps and shorter rest periods. This type of training is crucial in sports requiring considerable endurance and repetitive actions such as those used in soccer.

Hypertrophy phase   This phase usually occurs in the preseason and is usually a period where the athlete returns to her normal level of muscle mass after the off-season. Training during this phase consists of resistance training using 8 to 12 reps.

Strength phase This period prepares the athlete for competition. It also occurs in the preseason and is marked by training periods involving heavy loads of five to eight reps and slightly longer rest periods (longer than during endurance or hypertrophy) within each set.

Power phase This is a short phase that occurs in the preseason or during the competitive season. It is sometimes referred to as the peaking stage. Resistance training in this phase is marked by its explosive movement patterns and ability to generate force. Workouts consist of three to five reps with relatively long rest.

Peaking phase During this period the athlete peaks for a particular event or series of events like playoffs. Resistance training consists of maxing or testing the athlete. Exercises consist of one to three reps. This phase is often referred to as the neurological component, because during this period the neurological system establishes better pathways and optimal recruitment patterns to perform the specific task at hand.

Recovery phase This rest period can consist of days completely off or active rest and is often called detraining. Extremely fit athletes are not likely to lose conditioning during this phase. Instead, this phase provides additional recovery and rebuilding that may not be possible during regular training. For example, baseball coaches build mini recovery periods into their particularly long season. Then, at the end of the competitive season they schedule a longer period of time off.

Transition phase This phase serves the same purpose as recovery and is preferred over a complete layoff from exercise. Transition smoothly connects one period of training to the next through a series of workouts. These workouts would be the pre-hab exercises and general body-weight exercises such as agilities. For the athlete, we use pre-hab training and active rest to keep the body from declining, by giving it a chance to recover and even strengthen some of the injury prone areas. We also found that agility training for seniors and the general population makes a great training tool.

Sets, reps, resistance Every type of training requires a number of sets, reps, and the amount of resistance, or load. Specific seasons or periods are defined by the number of sets and reps and the resistance used during that training period.

Volume Volume is expressed as the number of sets times the number of reps. You can also include the amount of weight (sets times reps times weight). Athletes typically reduce the volume as they approach the competitive season of the peaking phase.

Rest Rest is probably the most important and most neglected aspect of training. Without giving your body time to adapt to and recover from a set or a workout, you will not progress optimally. Unless you're working on endurance, you must rest between sets during an activity period. You must also take adequate rest between sessions that work a particular muscle group.

Table 9.1 summarizes the set and rep combos for each of the desired training periods.

Table 9.1 Set and Rep Combos

	Hypertrophy	Strength	Power	Peaking
Sets	1–4	2–4	3–6	1–3
Reps	10–12	4–8	2–5	1–2
Volume	High	High	Low	Low
Intensity	Low	High	High	Maximal

Reprinted, by permission, from M.H. Stone, H. O'Bryant, & J. Garhammer, 1981, A hypothetical model for strength training, *Journal of Sports Medicine*, 21, 344.

DESIGNING A PERIODIZATION PROGRAM

With the definitions in hand, you're ready to design a periodized program. Before beginning a training program you must make sure you have achieved a base level of fitness. If not, begin a four- to eight-week base training routine. At the very least, work on shoulder and ankle strength so that you can safely perform the resistance workouts. Following are the steps to designing a training program:

Explosive Olympic lifters regularly use a periodized approach to training.

1. Map out the weeks and months of your competitive season.

2. Because most of the in-season workouts will be maintenance, build your program around the in-season time line.

3. Your preseason training program is the most crucial. Start by determining how long it will take to prepare for the season. Twelve weeks is usually sufficient, but this period can be longer if you have the time.

4. Next, use the remaining time for off-season training. If this period is short, rest or rehab is usually the training mode. If you find you have more than eight weeks of off-season, extend your preseason.

5. Once your main seasons are broken into weeks, split up those periods based on your training goals. Specific workouts should last no more than six weeks (although some coaches and researchers have found that as many as eight and as few as four are optimal). Specifically, four to five weeks is the suggested number when it comes to power. For strength training phases, up to eight weeks have shown to be effective. If your sport is at one end of the continuum, you will probably use longer cycles for those goals associated with your sport (8 to 12 weeks). If your sport lies closer to the middle, you will benefit from shorter phases (four to five weeks) to meet your training goals. Begin to build the mesocycles and microcycles based on the goals for each period.

6. Build a rest or decreased volume week into each mesocycle.

Now that you have your phases, it's time for the hard part. What do you do, and how long do you do it, and most important, at what intensity should you perform the exercises? Probably the most difficult part of any training program is picking the specific exercises. Because there are many good exercises and many things you would like to accomplish within a week or even a single workout, it is essential to know what your goals are for each season, each phase, each workout, and even each exercise, then zero in on the exercises that will help you reach those goals.

Building the perfect program takes years of experience. However, if you're new to sports or coaching, the following information will give you a good head start. You will be able to design a sound program that will reap results. Then over time, you will determine which configuration of phases and which exercises work best for you and further refine your program.

Determining Which Exercises to Use

To determine the appropriate exercise and intensity for each phase, consider the movements used in the sport and where the phase falls within the training year. The previous chapters provide descriptions of exercises appropriate for specific sports. In addition, your answers to the following questions will help you choose exercises:

1. What athletic activity besides weight training are you doing during this time period?

2. What type of recovery do you need before the next workout or practice? For example, a lower-body resistance workout on the day of or the day before an intense lower-body practice may not allow enough recovery.

3. Is your technique good enough to properly perform the exercise, or do you need to work on technique?

4. If your technique is sound, then concentrate on developing your weakest attributes (such as balance, quickness, etc.).

5. Have you performed simple exercises before moving on to more complex skills during the workout?

Determining Weight

There are two methods for determining the appropriate weight for a workout. You can determine the weight based on a percentage of one repetition max (%1RM). For example, if your maximum lift in the bench press is 150 pounds and you want to work out at 80 percent of 1RM, your workout weight is 120 pounds. Use table 9.2 to calculate the number of reps you should do at a percentage of 1RM. The table only goes up to 12 reps because percent-based training doesn't work well for more than 12 reps.

Or you can determine how much weight to lift in an exercise by looking up the rep range for the phase in table 9.2, then use as much weight as you can to complete that number of reps. This method allows you to do each exercise full out, completing the prescribed number of reps using the heaviest weight you can.

Table 9.2   %1RM Rep Prediction Chart

Relative %1RM	Number of reps that can be performed
100	1
95	2
92.5	3
90	4
87.5	5
85	6
82.5	7
80	8
75	10
70	12

Although many advocates of periodization prefer to use the %1RM, and each method has its advantages, if you believe in the overload theory, then maximal weight is the way to go. And in my opinion, using a percentage of 1RM presents more cons than pros. Although this method provides gradual progression, it fails to take advantage of overload. Although you can argue that maximal effort does not follow the gradual progressive overload theory, this argument is nullified by the fact that an entire periodized cycling plan is a gradual progression. It is not necessary to progress by a percentage of 1RM within each phase. Preset training does not allow the athlete to maximize his or her training day. Furthermore, you can easily progress your next workout off your last workout (like today you did 50 pounds, next workout you will use 55 pounds); therefore, it is not necessary to plan exactly how much you should do. If you plan your reps, sets, rest, etc. and work maximally for the given set, then why potentially limit or not attain your workout goals? Second, if the results of the 1RM test are inaccurate, then the entire periodized program will be off. The 1RM value may be skewed if the athlete tested poorly or if the tester skewed the results by recording values incorrectly, measuring incorrectly, but more likely, not ensuring proper technique, range of motion (ROM), etc. during testing, then forcing it during training. Another problem with this method is that some athletes max very well, but have difficulty performing 5 to 10 reps at the prescribed percentage. And finally, as the athlete gets stronger, she needs to establish a new 1RM or the values will be off. Although 1RM testing may be favored, it is not recommended more than three times per year (unless the sport requires it). Sports such as weightlifting, powerlifting, shot put, discus, possibly high jump, long jump, pole vault, etc., require more frequent testing.

It's important to remember to choose your exercises and intensity based on the needs of your sport. For example, percentage-based training may be better suited for sports consisting of a series of one-time explosive events less frequently, like powerlifting, weightlifting, and the throwing events in track and field. On the other hand, resistance training for sports such as any longer duration continuous sport such as cycling, distance running, or swimming doesn't require you to perform 1RM or even three reps at near maximal loads. Therefore, determining the number of reps and completing them all out may be the best method for determining what weight to use.

Intensity and Load Volume

Intensity has several meanings in the gym. In general terms, it means pushing yourself hard during a workout. However, its scientific meaning refers to amount of resistance or load used. And *load volume* expresses intensity as a function of the rest interval; as the rest interval changes, so does the intensity of the set.

The specific load volume can be expressed as an intensity-to-rest (IR) ratio, or the relationship between the rest and intensity of the given work set. Intensity is a function of the rest time between consecutive bouts and even consecutive workouts. Your workload for a specific task such as running, swimming, or resistance training is largely determined by the amount of rest between sets. For multiple-set workouts or interval workouts the load decreases, remains the same, or increases as the rest changes. Further, that load depends on the previous set's intensity as a percentage of the maximum effort per set.

Maximum intensity refers to the maximum weight possible for the entire set of reps. If your set requirement is to complete eight reps, the intensity would be equal to 100 percent if on the eighth rep you failed or needed help to complete it. This is different than lifting a percentage of your maximum (80 percent 1RM for eight reps), unless that percentage corresponds to your maximum amount for that set (you reach the failure point). In the IR concept, the term intensity describes the maximum resistance or speed attainable for the duration of the activity (could be a set or time, etc.).

The idea behind load volume is that you lift or exercise at your maximum level for the entire duration of the set, whether it is timed or determined by the number of reps. The recovery process during that rest period and the amount of recovery, both physical and mental, will determine the load for the subsequent set. Therefore, the load volume would be the amount of resistance (or speed) you use for each set. In fact, if you were to exert 100-percent effort on every set, then in all likelihood, the following sets would require a decrease in the intensity (even with sufficient rest). This philosophy is in stark contrast to the idea of progressing the resistance (and thus the intensity) with each consecutive set.

In chapter 7 we learned that anaerobic depletion of the phosphagen system occurs rapidly. We also know that as anaerobic glycolysis takes over, lactic acid is produced. As phosphagen usage increases, fatigue sets in. Furthermore, the production of lactic acid inhibits enzyme activity and possibly neural activity, which also results in fatigue. Rest is the key to replenishing phosphagen stores. Phosphagens can be restored to near maximum levels within three minutes. Rest, especially active rest, helps rid the body of lactic acid. Therefore, it is important that rest intervals correspond to the intensity and goal for the workout.

Figure 9.1 illustrates the relationship between intensity and rest. If the rest is too short, intensity cannot be maximal. And if the rest is too long, you will lose the "warmed up" effect from the previous sets and be unable to achieve maximal intensity. Ideally 3 minutes is the rest time but a well-conditioned athlete may rest far less, or in specific cases with some of the throwing events and lifting events, rest may be much greater (near 10 to 15 minutes). When determining the optimal amount of rest, you must consider the requirements of your sport. If your sport does not include rest periods of two minutes or more, then training should not include long rest periods.

Conditioning specifically for your sport will shift the intensity–time curve. A shift toward the left (dashed line B in figure 9.1) requires repeated bouts at high intensity with less rest. This shift is the result of better lactic acid tolerance and clearance and also greater phosphagen stores and quicker ATP-CP replenishment. A leftward shift, or greater load volume, is desirable for most sports. A

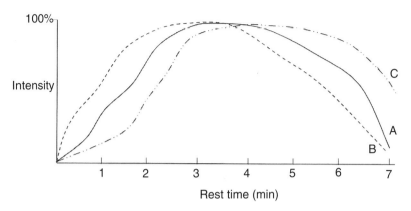

FIGURE 9.1 *The relationship between intensity and rest.*

shift toward the right (dashed–dotted line C in figure 9.1) is desirable in events where the athlete has several minutes between bouts of explosive activity, such as the long jump or weightlifting. The middle curve in figure 9.1 (dashed–dotted line A) represents a general training methodology practiced by most.

Efficiency also affects the rest period, and therefore intensity. As you are able to perform a task more efficiently, the task requires less energy, which delays fatigue and the subsequent breakdown in technique.

Table 9.3 outlines the energy requirements for particular sport categories. The more aerobic your sport, the less rest you take between longer sets. The opposite is true for anaerobic sports.

Once you have determined the energy requirements of your sport, your conditioning program will be based on that overall energy demand. During the preseason, the rest times and set duration should be similar to competition situations. For example, because a baseball player is inactive for long periods, but must periodically produce a rapid rotation swing and a brief sprint, rest between sets can be long, and the set should consist of three to six reps or last less than 10 seconds as the season nears.

Periodized Model

A typical periodized model will look something like figure 9.2 on page 208. The sample periodization model illustrates a general resistance training progression. Of course, if your sport is more speed based, strength based, or power based, your training program will reflect that.

Volume of Training

A constant question on every athlete's mind is if the training program includes enough work. The old adage "no pain, no gain" is constantly challenged by "quality, not quantity." One way to safely tread this line is to make sure the quality of the exercises aren't sacrificed for the sake of quantity.

Table 9.3 Energy Requirements for Various Sports

Sport	ATP-PC%	ATP-LA%	Aerobic%
Baseball	85	10	5
Basketball	60	30	10
Football (three plays out)	90	10	0 (very little)
Football (several plays)	75	20	5
Hockey	60	30	10
Soccer	30	30	40
Volleyball	85	10	5
Rowing	20	30	50
Wrestling	10	65	25
Boxing	10	60	30
Tennis	70	20	10
Golf	95	5	0 (very little)
Swimming 50 m	95	5	0 (very little)
Swimming 100 m	80	15	5
Swimming 200 m	35	60	5
Swimming 400 m	20	40	40
Swimming 1000+ m	5	25	70
Diving	98	2	0 (very little)
Sprinting 60 m	100	0 (very little)	0 (very little)
Sprinting 100 m	98	2	0 (very little)
Sprinting 200 m	60–65	30–35	0 (very little)
Sprinting 400 m	40	60	0 (very little)
Running 800 m	30	65	5
Running 1500 m	20	40	40
Running 3 K	10	20	70
Running 5-15 K	5	15	80
Marathon +	0 (very little)	10–15	85–90
Walking	0 (very little)	5	95
Long/High Jump	98	2	0 (very little)
Rollerblading (regular)	5	15	80
Bicycling (regular)	5	15	80

Upper body, lower body combo, 2 – 3x/wk 1 – 2 sets			Upper body, lower body separate, 2x/wk 1 – 3 sets		Split routine such as chest, tris – back, bis – legs 1 – 2x/wk each 2 – 3 sets		Variety, upper/lower combo 1x/wk, then split routines 1 – 3 sets			

IV												
R	12–15	10–12	10–12	8–10	6–8	6–8	4–6	6–8	8–10	8–10	6–8	8–10
I	Low	Mod	Mod	High	High	High	High	High	Mod	High	High	Mod
V	Low	Low	Mod	Mod	High	Mod	Low	High	Low	Mod	Mod	High
	Jan	Feb	Mar	Apr	May	Jun	Jul	Aug	Sep	Oct	Nov	Dec
	The first week of every month is a recovery week–decrease V and I											
	Progression			Loading–Recovery–Loading						Maintenance		

R = reps; I = relative intensity; V = volume; IV = intensity times volume

FIGURE 9.2   Periodized model.

To make sure the workload is appropriate, be sure your coach watches you while you work out. If you have a tough time staying focused or keeping up with the demand of the session, then you must increase the rest or reduce the overall volume. Tell-tale signs that it's time to stop a particular exercise or even the entire session are the inability to maintain proper posture, the inability to jump at a minimum of 75 percent of maximal effort, the inability to make crisp, clean cuts in agility drills or performing them at much slower speeds than usual, and the inability to complete the required number of reps in a resistance workout. In all these cases, the risk of injury or improper neural conditioning outweighs the benefits of continuing the exercise.

Often coaches confuse conditioning with training. When it comes to building power, every rep must be explosive, and every rep must be executed with precision. Athletes tend to use poor technique in conditioning exercises, which is fine, but drills should be both clearly explained to the athlete and understood where they fit in the program.

Cycling a Program

Progression, moving through each season toward the end goal, is a complicated process. A systematic approach and meticulous record keeping will help you build the perfect training program over the years. Within each phase you need specific instructions for reaching the overall training goal. Additionally, the training program during each phase must mesh with the training goal or the specific requirements of the sport. Figure 9.3 shows the breakdown of each season or cycle as it falls in the entire macrocycle.

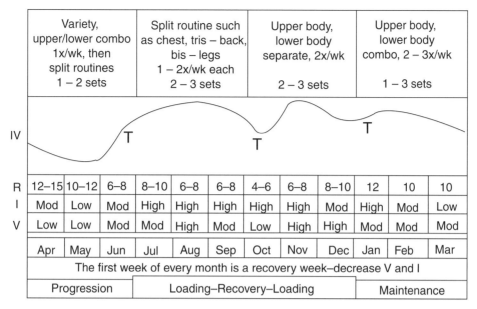

R	12–15	10–12	6–8	8–10	6–8	6–8	4–6	6–8	8–10	12	10	10
I	Mod	Low	Mod	High	High	High	High	High	Mod	High	Mod	Low
V	Low	Low	Mod	Mod	High	Mod	Low	High	High	Mod	Mod	Mod
	Apr	May	Jun	Jul	Aug	Sep	Oct	Nov	Dec	Jan	Feb	Mar

The first week of every month is a recovery week–decrease V and I

Progression	Loading–Recovery–Loading	Maintenance

T = testing

FIGURE 9.3 Macrocycle.

Cycling within the macrocycle   Within the yearlong training program, the athlete must reduce volume at times to enhance recovery, which allows a greater overall training effect. In figure 9.3, the intensity–volume curve undulates, showing progressive intensity increases at the transition from the in-season phase to off-season and moving to the preseason. The loading phases represent periods where the intensity and volume are highest and maintained (figure 9.4). These loading phases are usually part of the preseason or preseason phase. Recovery is built into the program.

Cycling within the mesocycle   During each three- to four-month time period, it is necessary to allow the body to adapt to the training. Notice how the intensity–volume curve takes a sharp decline every four to six weeks (see figure 9.4). Typically, each four to eight weeks you must change at least one aspect of volume (intensity or number of sets or reps), otherwise you will become stale. However, in the case of younger or less experienced athletes, the training effect and rate of improvement may not fall off for 12 or more weeks. An intentional reduction in intensity or volume enhances the recovery and adaptation process.

Weekly cycles   Within each training week (figure 9.5), it may be important to include a day of basic lifts, even when training specifically for power and speed as this will help maintain overall strength. The same may be true when training for pure strength. To do this, plan the week so that basic resistance training is combined with the more specific resistance training into a single-day combined upper- and lower-body routine placed at the end of the week or after the major explosive work is done. This would also be a good time to perform the complex training from chapter 7. This notion works well with a strength athlete as well.

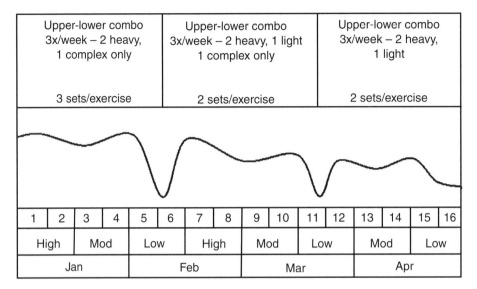

FIGURE 9.4 *Mesocycle.*

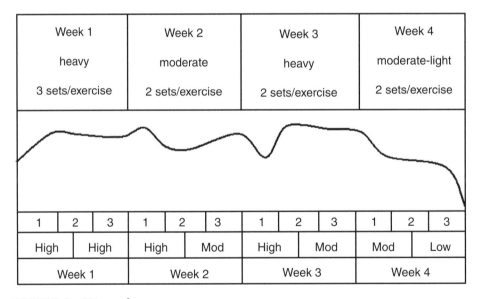

FIGURE 9.5 *Microcycle.*

From time to time it may be necessary to change the stimulus by adding a speed day into the weekly cycle.

Lowering the intensity or volume by workout or week Many coaches and athletes do not understand the concept of a reduced-work week and do not employ them for fear of losing speed or strength. Off days and weeks are needed, even when soreness is not present. The term *off* should not be confused with *do nothing*, unless complete rest is necessary. Instead, in an off week reduce the amount of weight used, reduce the number of reps, or decrease the overall work done in a single day to enhance recovery. In some cases you may just drop one workout out of the week. Remember too, although heavy plyometrics, agility drills, and speed work do not produce the same delayed-onset muscle soreness as resistance training, you must also reduce their volume periodically.

Volume Training As a Modality

Volume training, a somewhat controversial training method, can be effective in developing a "never say die" attitude. However, it must be used sparingly and only at certain times during the training year. The concept of volume training is quite simple: Overload the system with as much stimulus as possible so that the sheer volume of the exercises alone triggers a physiological and, probably more important, psychological response that will help you endure the rigors of sport. Or to put it simply, you need quantity, quantity, and more quantity.

Ideally, the watchword of any training program is quality; however, when undertaking volume training, you are allowed to continue when quality deteriorates if you can do the exercise safely. Typically, the challenge of volume training is motivation. You must learn to tolerate the pain and fatigue of lactic acid buildup, and continue to compete physically and mentally. When used in team sports, you learn to support your teammates through encouragement and to trust that they won't let you down.

If you choose to attempt volume training it must be carefully planned. Use it sparingly and only during the off-season or in a rare preseason burst. Don't use it during the season or a specific training cycle. Choose exercises that are easy to execute. Typically, these are single-joint movements or body-weight exercises such as biceps curls and push-ups. Loading the volume on a fairly complex multijoint exercise such as the free-bar squat for extended sets and reps will sacrifice form and ultimately lead to injury.

You can increase the volume of an exercise in three ways. You can increase the number of sets to as many as 10 or 12. You can increase the number of reps to as many as 20 or 30. Or you can shorten the rest period and extend both the sets and reps. The first method takes too much time and you will become bored before becoming fatigued. If you want to increase the reps, use drop sets. Start with a weight that can be done for about eight reps, then drop off about 20 to 30 percent and go until fatigued, then continue to drop another 20 to 30 percent for two more sets and lighten the load as required. If you start with a very light resistance you could end up doing more than 50 reps. The best choice for volume training is to extend the exercise to about six sets of about 20 reps each, with a rest period of no more than 45 seconds. Primarily because of lactic acid buildup, fatigue will occur rapidly.

The set ends when your coach decides that your form has deteriorated to a predetermined point. This process allows you to exercise continually, achieving a large total exercise volume. Form will suffer only slightly, and you will develop a resistance to lactic acid. But most important, you will develop the attitude and commitment required to endure every play during an overtime game.

Another way to achieve volume is to challenge yourself between normal exercise sets. In other words, you could "circuit style" your workout for several exercises after your main exercises are completed. For example, you could perform a set of crunches between exercises, or if it's a leg day, do squats or leg presses, leg extensions, and leg curls with proper rest, then go to lunges (single or both legs) or body-weight squats until failure for several sets with very little rest. Or you could "burn out" ("burn out" meaning an extended set—maybe 20 to 30 reps—that you may need to use the drop training method to achieve) doing leg extensions. All of these alternatives increase the volume of your workout. Another way to increase volume is superslow sets of sustained tension.

The key to volume training is *volume*. This does not mean that the workout must last several hours, but that an individual session must consist of a tremendous amount of work.

SPEED AND STRENGTH CYCLES

Using the speed–strength continuum, you can develop a power training program by cycling training through phases of speed and strength development. However, rather than using specific periods such as endurance, hypertrophy, or strength, your periods are derived from the continuum: pure strength, strength-speed, pure speed, speed-strength, and pure power (see figure 9.6).

Ideally, you can try to train both speed and strength during a single session; however, it is best to periodize the program by concentrating on a single aspect at a time to allow individual recovery and proper adaptation. Trying to train too many things such as speed and strength concurrently in a single workout will decrease the effect of each. Keep in mind that depending on your sport (such as football or any sport within the speed-strength category), some aspects will overlap. A program that trains each aspect separately would progress like the models in figure 9.7.

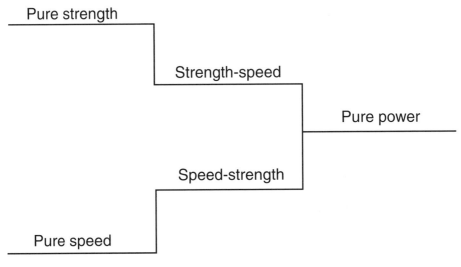

FIGURE 9.6 *Ideal periodized training model.*

Table 9.4 outlines an 18-week program with each period lasting three to four weeks. It represents a typical training program for developing power. This is not necessarily the cycling method for a football, basketball, or soccer player. Instead it shows what the progression through a program could look like.

Training for power is complicated, especially when you consider that most sports require speed, strength, and endurance. When endurance is not a factor, the true power scenario outlined in table 9.4 may work well. Otherwise, you must modify this general model to meet the requirements of your sport. For

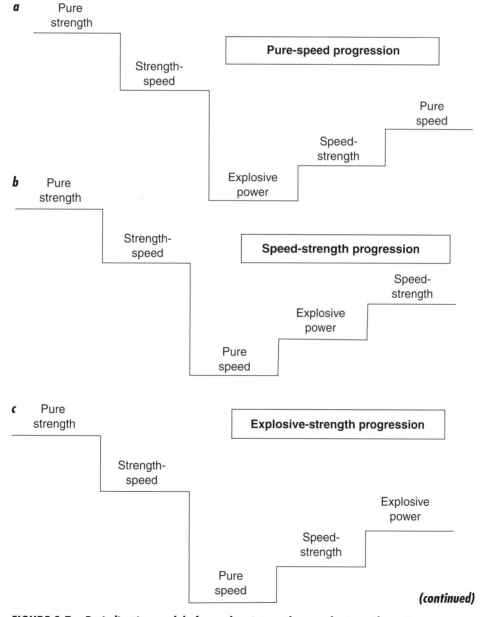

(continued)

FIGURE 9.7 *Periodization models for each point on the speed–strength continuum.*

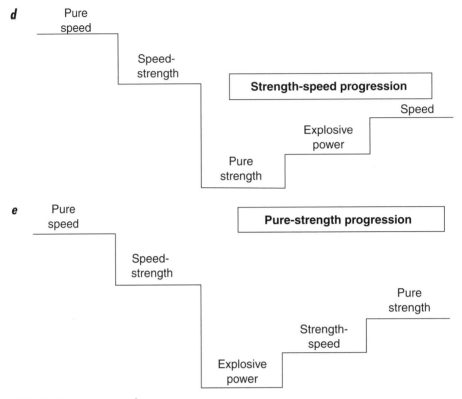

FIGURE 9.7 *(continued)*

Table 9.4 Power-Peaking Program

Phase	Pure strength	Strength-speed	Pure speed	Speed-strength	Pure power
Sets	3	5	3	5	4
Reps	8	6	8	6	3-5
Weight (relative%)	8RM 80–85	8RM* 70–75	50RM* 10–20	25RM 25–35	12RM 40–60
Rest (min)	2-3	3	3	3	4
Weeks	4	3	4	3	3-4

*This is a relative value, meaning that weight used should be very light relative to strength.

example, for team sports, you might shorten each phase to one or two weeks due to seasonal time constraints (practices, school, etc.).

The key to setting up an effective periodized program is to know what you want to achieve. Once you have set your goal, you can start building your program. The next chapter teaches you to monitor and modify your periodized program.

10

Monitoring and Adjusting Your Training

Training without monitoring your progress is like driving with your eyes closed: You *will* get somewhere, but you can't be sure that where you end up is where you wanted to be, and you can't be sure what shape you'll be in when you get there. Monitoring your training daily allows you to adjust your program so that you can progress and recover as quickly as possible.

CHARTING YOUR WORKOUTS

A training logbook is one of the best investments you can make. In the logbook you will keep records of what occurs during training sessions and why. A logbook is a space to record all the data you need, as well as observations and recovery information.

Your logbook does not have to be fancy. In fact, the less complex it is, the more information you will be able to record. Standard workout charts have spaces to record sets and reps within designated columns, but they don't leave room for additional information that may describe how the set really went. For

© Empics

Every type of athlete, including swimmers, should use a logbook to monitor their progress in workouts.

example, let's look at a set of six reps. In one workout you are able to do eight on your own rather than six. During another workout you only do four on your own, and your partner helps you through six. Both of these scenarios require more explanation than simply one set of six reps. Or what if your workout is three sets of six reps, and on the first set you complete six, on the second you complete five, and on the third, you only do four on your own. How do you record this on a typical chart?

The more information you can record on your workout card, the more information you have to help you plan the next workout. I know several strength coaches who have saved every record of every workout their athletes have done since they began coaching (some have coached more than 15 years). They use this information to plan the progressions for their athletes. Logging and recording workouts is vital to designing a proper periodized workout. Table 10.1 shows how most people record a week's worth of strength workouts. Notice how difficult it is to see what happened on a particular day because all three training days are recorded on the same chart regardless of which parts of the body were worked. And this data provides little information about the quality of each set.

Although this chart provides a fine overview of the workout week, it does not tell you what actually happened. Table 10.2 on page 218 provides far more information and separates the program into a single workout per page. Then, when comparing your workouts from week to week, you can compare the same body parts and movements, rather than looking only at what you did over the

Table 10.1   Typical Logbook

Exercise name	Date	Number of sets	Number of reps	Weight used (lbs)
Bench press	2–3	3	8	135
Incline press	2–3	2	10	100
Pec deck	2–3	2	12	60
Shoulder press	2–5	3	6	90
Shoulder raise	2–5	2	10	15
Triceps push-down	2–3	3	10	55
Ab crunch	2–3	2	25	
Pull-up	2–7	2	8	
Lat pull-down	2–7	3	10	120
Seated row	2–7	2	8	140
Straight bar curl	2–7	3	12	45
Leg press	2–5	4	10	175
Leg extension	2–5	2	12	65
Leg curl	2–5	2	12	45
Standing calf	2–5	3	15	200
Seated calf	2–5	2	15	75
Low back extension	2–7	1	12	80

1 lb = .45 kg

week. By comparing similar workout days, you can spot improvement over the four- to eight-week period much more easily. The page should be set up in a landscape (horizontal) orientation to provide maximum room for comments.

This chart makes information about exercise performance readily available. And more important, if you must make changes, last week's workout is right in front of you, so you don't have to try to remember what you did last week on the bench press. This method requires more time; however, the help it provides for projecting the proper weight and reps for subsequent workouts is worth the effort.

Numbers

In addition to recording the number of sets, reps, and weight used in a strength training session, many athletes use their logbooks to make sure they have completed all the activities in a training session. Both of these benefits are important; your logbook can become a powerful training tool.

Table 10.2 Detailed Logbook

Exercise	Week 1	Week 2	Week 3	Week 4
Warm-up Bench press	1 × 8 × 100 1 × 6 × 135	1 × 8 × 100 1 × 6 × 135	1 × 8 × 100 1 × 6 × 135	1 × 8 × 100 1 × 6 × 135
Bench press	2 × 8 × 185 1 × 6 × 185	2 × 8 × 185 1 × 8 × 185 +1	3 × 8 × 185	1 × 8 × 195 1 × 7 × 195 1 × 6 × 195 +1
Incline press	2 × 10 × 65 (DB) 2 × 8 × 65 (DB)	2 × 10 × 65 (DB) 1 × 9 × 65 (DB)	3 × 10 × 65 (DB)	2 × 10 × 70 (DB) 1 × 9 × 65 (DB)
Dip Pec deck	1 × 10 × 60 1 × 10 × 60 +1 1 × 9 × 60	3 × 10 × 60	1 × 10 × 65 1 × 9 × 65 1 × 9 × 60*	Could not do today because shoulder was too sore
Triceps movement	3 × 12 × 65 head cavers	2 × 10 × 80 1 × 8 × 80 push-down	1 × 10 × 60/40/20 1 × 10 × 50/30/20 1 × 8 × 50/30/20	3 × 10 × 60
Lateral shoulder raise	2 × 12 × 50 machine	2 × 12 × 15 (DB)	1 × 12 × 60 machine 1 × 12 × 20 (DB)	Did not do, shoulder was too sore
Ab crunch**	3 × 25	1 × 25 1 × 10 × 25 1 × 10 × 15	2 × 15 × 25 1 × 15 × 15	3 × 15 × 25

1 lb = .45 kg
DB = dumbbell
+1 = additional rep with spotter's help
50/30/20 (notation used to indicate that weight was reduced and set was extended)
* Chose 60-lb dumbbells because shoulder was bothering me
** Ab crunches done with additional weight

When training for power you will perform a variety of exercises from jumps and throws to various plyometrics and sprints, covering a range of speed and strength options. The numbers you gather must reflect the nature of the drill: the height or distance for throws and jumps and distance or time for sprints. These measurements provide concrete evidence of your progress and should be measured in every workout.

10 Percent Drop-Off Rule

Like resistance training with weights, plyometrics, throws, sprints, and other power exercises are planned using sets and reps. Strength training workout intensity is controlled by the amount of resistance. If 80 percent of 1RM is on the bar, the athlete will reach a failure point at 10 to 12 reps. However, you never perform plyometrics or throws to the point of muscular failure, which makes it more difficult to determine when you stop benefiting from the set. Guidelines for the number of jumps and throws in a training session are provided in chapter 7, but those are just guidelines based on a variety of athletes at various fitness levels with different recovery abilities. They provide a starting point for planning. But once you start training, you will individualize your program to meet your current fitness level, state of fatigue, and motivational level, and base the duration of a set on drops in power and energy (see chapter 7 for more).

Energy is the limiting factor in all power activities. The amount of energy you can produce determines the amount of and duration of the work you can achieve. During high-intensity plyometric activity the body relies primarily on the adenosine triphosphate and creatine phosphate (phosphagens) stored in the muscles for energy. The ATP-CP system is the most powerful energy system in the body, producing huge amounts of energy in a very short period of time. Unfortunately, phosphagen stores are limited; therefore, the energy system is quickly depleted, resulting in a drop in speed and power. The rate of depletion of the ATP-CP system depends on what drill you are doing, but you are generally limited to 5 to 15 seconds of continuous all-out work. As this energy system is depleted, your power output decreases, which causes a decrease in performance.

Power output below 90 percent of max will not create a speed or power training effect. Once power drops below 90 percent of max, you should stop the set. Determining this power drop is relatively easy, requiring only a stopwatch, measuring tape, calculator, and accurate records. Let's look at an example using a standing sidearm throw with a med ball or a ball with a handle to hold (power grip ball). After a good warm-up, place a mark on the ground and roll out a tape measure. Throw a power grip ball as far as you can and measure the throw. Repeat this for a total of four throws and record your best distance. Subtract 10 percent of this distance and place a mark on the ground at that point; this represents the minimum distance you need to obtain on each throw. When you fail to reach the 90-percent line on two consecutive reps, stop the set. After a short rest perform another set until you fail to reach the 90-percent line, then rest again. You may not achieve the same number of repetitions in each set. This is fine, because fatigue will carry over from set to set. As long as you perform at 90 percent of your best, you will achieve the speed and power training effect you want without taking your body to the fatigue point. Repeat this procedure until you reach the drop-off point.

The 10 percent drop-off system uses the best score on each training day. An alternative is to use a 10-percent drop from the best score obtained during a scheduled test session. The advantage is that after the test session, you only have to calculate 90 percent once, making it quicker and easier for coaches working with a large group of athletes. Unfortunately, relying on test results doesn't allow you to adjust the program for the improvements you make between test sessions. If you decide to use test results, schedule retests every four weeks. Be sure to test each exercise and drill you will use in the program.

Whether you base your 10 percent drop on test results or the best for each training session, you should schedule a formal test session every six to eight weeks to ensure that the program is delivering the desired results.

The 10 percent drop-off rule takes a little more organization and time to employ than looking up reps and sets on a chart, but it is well worth the extra effort to be able to adjust a program on the fly to avoid injury or to take advantage of a good day. After three to four weeks of using the drop-off rule, go back and compare the volume of work you accomplished to the volume prescribed in the program. If your volume over the three- to four-week period was greater than the prescribed volume, you have better recovery ability than the average athlete and can increase the volume of your training to the levels you found using the drop-off rule. If your volume was less than prescribed, decrease the training volume to meet your current physiological state. And don't worry, your volume will increase as your recovery ability improves. This volume reflects your current fitness, not your potential for improvement or performance.

Monitoring Recovery

Numbers are your friends when it comes to developing power. Recording sets, reps, speed, body weight, and time provides a basis for measuring and monitoring training sessions and the program as a whole. Numbers are not the whole story, however. They will tell you what is happening in a training session but won't explain why. You must combine training data with recovery data that measures sleep, soreness, and other physiological parameters to know whether you are heading toward an overtraining state or not.

Over the years many physiological tests have been developed to measure recovery and to guide training programs. Blood urea, creatine kinase, hormone levels and ratios, and blood amino acid profiles are just some of them. If you are a professional making millions of dollars per year or are a world-class athlete with access to an Olympic training center or other top medical and physiology labs and consultants, these tests are worthwhile. For everyone else there is a much simpler method that is just as effective as expensive blood work: the recovery questionnaire. Michael Kellmann and K. Wolfgang Kallus have developed and validated an extensive questionnaire that can be used in research studies and to monitor training, the *Recovery-Stress Questionnaire for Athletes,* published by Human Kinetics in 2001. This is an excellent tool for full-time athletes, but is too long for most athletes to use on a daily basis. A modified recovery questionnaire gives most athletes the information they need to assess their readiness for the day's training.

Recovery questionnaire Fill out the recovery questionnaire every day, even on a rest day. You want to measure the effect of a day off as well as a training day. Begin by establishing a two- to three-week baseline in the off-season when you are doing little or no training. The baseline is used to measure how far from a fully recovered state you are moving as a result of training. You will refer to it every week, so keep the baseline numbers handy.

Table 10.3   Recovery Questionnaire

Item	Mon	Tues	Wed	Thurs	Fri	Sat	Sun	Average	Baseline
Hours of sleep									
Sleep quality									
Muscle soreness									
Joint soreness									
General fatigue									
Desire to train									
Motivation									
Morning HR									
Body weight									

HR = heart rate

Rate each item in table 10.3 on a scale of 1 to 10, using half points and whole numbers. Low numbers are better. For example, a rating of 1 on sleep quality means you had a great night's sleep. A 10 means you were up most of the night. The ratings are based on how you feel when you first wake up and get out of bed in the morning. Be honest with yourself; you will use this information to adjust your program. Body weight should be measured after voiding and before breakfast so that conditions for the weigh-in are standardized. Morning heart rate is measured as soon as you wake up. Keep a watch by your bed and take a 30-second count and multiply it by two to get the number of beats per minute.

StrengthPro Inc. has developed an alternative to the recovery–stress questionnaire that can be used daily. You can develop your own set of questions; however, these seem best in helping gauge recovery and training adaptation while developing power.

Using the data to adjust the program   Throughout the training year you will compare all data to the baseline established in the off-season. No single variable can assess recovery; the power of the questionnaire comes from using multiple variables simultaneously. If you see an increase of two points over the baseline on three or more unshaded variables two days in a row, you need to take a day off or cut the volume and intensity of the day's training in half. If the week's average of three of the unshaded items increases by three or more points, you need to schedule a recovery week, even if you haven't planned one.

Morning heart rate and body weight are not included in the daily and weekly analysis because changes in these variables happen much more gradually than the other factors. Closely look at increases in morning heart rate of more than 10 beats per minute for a week or more. If your heart rate is elevated without changes in the other variables, you may be losing aerobic fitness, which may or may not affect your performance depending on the endurance demands of your sport. If your weekly averages in the unshaded variables are increasing and morning heart rate is elevated, consider planning a recovery week.

An unintentional decrease in body weight is an early sign of overtraining. Body weight can fluctuate daily because of hydration levels and what you ate and drank the previous day. Very large athletes can see their weight change by several pounds from day to day; because of this it is better to use weekly percent changes in body weight to assess your long-term weight profile. If you see an unintended weekly weight loss of more than two percent, you must make adjustments to your training or diet. First increase fluid intake to see if you are dehydrated. If the weekly average of other variables are increasing and your body weight is decreasing, there is a good chance that you are beginning to overtrain and need to schedule a recovery week. Monitoring increases in body weight is also important. For sports where body-weight classes exist, small changes in weight can make a big difference. For the rest of you, eating too much and increasing fat over lean muscle mass is an obvious disadvantage.

Adding observations Outside factors influence your ability to train. You need space to record training observations in your logbook. Observations help explain why you are feeling as you are and why training is going as it is. Record difficulties in your training and unusual events that may have an impact on your program. For instance, if you had a busy day of classes and skipped lunch, record this because it may affect an after-school training session. And if it occurs regularly, recognizing this pattern will help you adjust your workout on days you miss lunch. Things to keep track of include, but are not limited to: activity in addition to training such as physical education classes, biking or walking to workouts, pickup games with friends, and physical jobs; eating schedules and amounts; and work assignments, exams, family commitments, and other events that disrupt your normal schedule and increase the stress in your life. As you evaluate changes in your recovery questionnaire, these observations will help you determine if your training program or an outside cause is impairing your recovery and progress. Armed with this knowledge, you can make appropriate adjustments.

Other Adjustments to the Program

The periodized program that you develop in the off-season is a road map for the training year. Occasionally detours and other unforeseen events like injury, work or school commitments, and family issues force you to stray from your intended path, requiring a change in the program. If you are forced to lay off because of injury or events beyond your control, you need a plan for getting back onto your regular schedule.

In the event of a minor injury, the best option is to train around the injury, doing as much of the regular program as possible without further aggravating the injured area. This will return you to your scheduled program quickly with a minimal loss of strength and power. If the injury forces you to miss training or competitions and limits your ability to do other workouts, you will need to modify your training program. But first you must get approval to return to regular training, most likely sometime after you are pain free and have undergone basic rehabilitation work. Next, you must reassess your power profile using the tests in chapter 2. This will tell you how much speed, strength, and power you lost as a result of the injury and where you need to focus your training. A short three- to four-week period of base building followed by a three- to four-week cycle of maximum strength training should get you back into your regular schedule of power development.

Of course, this scenario assumes that the injury occurred late in the training year. If you are injured early in the year, to adjust the program take the number of weeks lost from injury and subtract them from the training year. Then replan the year using the adjusted number of weeks. For instance, if you lose six weeks because of injury you will now base your year on 46 weeks rather than 52.

Hard work and the dedication to a periodized program pays off with individual or team victory.

TESTING YOUR PROGRESS

Most sports use some sort of fitness testing during training camp to assess the abilities of each athlete. Many athletes view testing as the coach's way of seeing whether they trained in the off-season or not. What few athletes realize and fewer coaches are willing to admit is that formalized fitness testing is as much a test of the coach's training program as it is the athlete's dedication and work ethic. Repeating testing at regular intervals throughout the season provides both coach and athlete valuable information on the overall success of the training program and the athlete's progress toward her goals.

Chapter 2 provides a series of tests recommended as the starting point for developing your program. These tests help you determine the types of speed and strength and in what proportions you should develop them to create the power profile for your sport according to the speed–strength continuum. Perform these tests at the start of the off-season, preseason, and postseason to monitor your progress toward your ideal power profile. Sport-specific performance and fitness tests like the 40-yard dash in football or home-to-second sprint in baseball should be conducted every eight weeks throughout the year. You will not see or expect to see progress at every test session because of the differences in focus at various times in the year. However, the tests will ensure that you do not experience detraining or loss of speed, strength, and power.

If you test during the competitive season, do it carefully. And avoid testing in the two to three weeks before a major competition or championship game. Testing close to a major competition does not provide enough time to adjust the program to correct weaknesses or problems, and poor test results are common at this time of year in individual sports where athletes only compete in a few key competitions each year. At this time of year, fatigue is high because of the intense training and competition schedule prior to the major taper of the year. A poor test can be psychologically devastating to a team or individual. Athletes may start to question their preparation and the coach's ability to develop a championship program, leading to a negative mindset going into the most important competition of the year.

Using Workouts to Monitor Progress

Formalized test sessions are great tools for monitoring training and the athlete's response to pressure situations. They can be a nice break from regular practice schedules, and if handled properly by a coaching staff, can be used to build team cohesion and morale. However, they are time consuming and require a day or two of decreased training so that everyone is well rested going into the session. This disrupts the training schedule, and testing can become a logistical nightmare for large teams. Several options are less intrusive and time consuming. A weekly logbook review is the simplest of the monitoring tools. You already know the numbers and recovery measures that should be recorded. Taking a few minutes at the end of each week to compare the results of the training session to previous weeks and months clearly shows if progress is occurring or not. If you are lifting more weight, running faster, jumping higher, or covering more distance, then your fitness is improving and the program is working. Progress won't be linear, so don't expect to see changes every workout or even every week if you are an elite athlete. But you should see signs of progress from training cycle to training cycle and in comparison to previous years. Recreational athletes that begin a power training program will see marked improvements over the first several weeks of training and in some cases even months after. Initial results tend to be inflated due to the process of neurological recruitment. The longer you have been working out, the harder you have to work to continue to see gains. On a good note however, it is far easier to maintain, stay in overall good health and shape, when you have been training for a longer period of time.

You must also monitor your training to make sure that the gains you are making are appropriate for the stage you are in. For instance, if you are trying to improve your sport-specific speed and power, but are seeing increases in the weight you can lift in the weight room, you should look at your strength maintenance program to see if it is too intense. You should maintain strength during this stage, not build it. A program intense enough to build strength may deplete energy reserves and effort that you should dedicate to sport-specific training. Table 10.4 shows the expected training adaptations in each of the steps in the program.

Table 10.4   Training Adaptations in Each Step

Step	Expected adaptations	Maintained abilities
Base building	Strengthen connective tissue	Reduced injury
Maximizing strength	Increase strength	Base speed and strength
Developing explosive acceleration	Increase speed and footwork	Gained strength
Combining speed and strength	Balance coordination, skill, and power	Speed and strength
Transferring training to performance	Increase power and movement timing	Speed and strength

Challenge Workouts

A second method for monitoring progress through workouts is to schedule challenge workouts. These are informal weekly testing sessions where one to three exercises are performed for maximum weight, reps, speed, or distance or are performed for time. The challenge exercises are normally scheduled exercises or drills, and they are performed as they come up in the scheduled workout. Coaches should be on hand to track results, and the winner of the day's challenge can be determined either based on improvement, absolute performance, or a combination of both. Posting the results on the team's bulletin board can motivate athletes to put forth full effort and to take the challenges seriously. Challenge workouts can be planned at any time and work best if they are announced the day before.

You spend hours and hours training toward very specific performance goals. Therefore, it's imperative that you monitor the effectiveness of your program and improvements in fitness to ensure that each training session creates a positive adaptation and that valuable training time is not wasted on ineffective or poorly timed workouts. Effective use of a logbook and regularly planned testing sessions are monitoring tools that will help you see when it's time to adjust your program to your level of fitness, recovery ability, and mental state.

With your periodized training plan in hand and a way to track your results and monitor your improvements, you are ready to build a program. The next chapter discusses how to build specific programs and how to build your end product.

11

Sample Exercise Programs

Developing the ideal program for your particular sport is truly a labor of love. It takes many years for strength coaches to develop their final product and most continue to change their programs regularly as newer training methods evolve.

You now have a set of tools to design your own program and/or modify the ones I have provided. There is no one perfect program or one specific training method that has proven more successful than another. The simple fact is that your approach to your workout and/or your athlete's workout may be more important than the workout itself!

The following programs are designed for four to six weeks of training and then progress through to additional workouts along the continuum according to the progressions set in chapter 9 (figure 9.7 on page 213). Workouts that focus primarily on the upper or lower body can be combined or alternated during a week, unless you are trying to achieve a specific training goal that focuses on only one. While most athletes will work on their weight training and explosive training two to four times during the week, you can modify your training program to meet the demands of your season and practice schedule.

Remember, these workouts are designed around maximal effort training—you should be fatigued from each workout. Fatigue, however, does not necessarily mean out of breath, rather it usually refers to feeling spent, weak, and tired.

Before you begin one of the selected routines or your own, it is important to remember these points about training for power:

1. All out or else. If you do not go all out, you will not see the maximal benefits of power training. Anything less than 100-percent effort reduces the effectiveness of the exercises. Remember, it is not so much what you specifically do, rather it is how you perform it.

2. Rest is crucial. Rest is crucial for the success of true power development. While rest times between exercise sets may seem excessive at first, the rest will be needed if you are performing exercises all-out. Recall that rest allows for replenishment of energy, reduction of fatiguing metabolites, and rest for the neurological system. Three minutes is a minimum for true recovery and four to five minutes for optimal performance. Having said that, when time constraints are an issue, such as preseason or with hectic school and practice hours, reduced rest times can be used. But be aware that reducing the rest reduces the true maximal efforts after the first few sets. Additionally, novice trainees will not need as much rest at first while perfecting skills as full-out effort is not entirely built by this point. And finally, rest times can be reduced to match the conditioning effect you are trying to achieve and/or the time per play, between play, or event during your sport.

3. Combining workouts. When combining workouts be careful to select only a few exercises. You cannot achieve everything in a single workout or for that matter a single week. The idea of the four- to six-week training program is to allow yourself ample training for all of the components that make up that specific portion of the continuum that you are focusing on. Also, be sure that your upper body has fully recovered from the last workout before performing upper-body explosive training (same for the lower body).

4. Patience. Patience is truly a virtue and is needed with power training. At first when you do some of these workouts, you will not "feel" as though you have had a "killer" workout; that will change when you really get working hard. Also, results will not show immediately, nor should you try to "max out" or test your efforts during the training cycle. Changes will take place and need time to build (remember the house analogy).

Each workout is designed to focus on specific combinations; however, you should substitute exercises as you need to. If you are particularly weak in an area, then that should be the focus of your workout. The set and rep combinations are for intermediate-level athletes. Beginners can do less sets and advanced athletes can do more work sets. Warm-ups and technique/skill training should not count in the overall number of sets (that means that the set-rep guidelines are for maximal effort sets only). On that note, only maximal effort sets that are performed with proper technique should be counted.

PURE-STRENGTH WORKOUTS

Tempo on all exercises (table 11.1) is three to four seconds on eccentric. There is a one-second pause in between eccentric and concentric portions of a lift. The concentric portion is two to three seconds.

Table 11.1 *Pure-Strength Workouts*

	Sets	Reps	Rest (min)
Big Squat Workout			
Squat	5	5	5–6
Leg curl	3	8	3–4
Leg press	3	8	3–4
Leg curl	3	8	3–4
Calf raise	3	8	3–4
Big Bench Workout			
Bench	5	5	5–6
Inclined dumbbell bench	3	8	3–4
Dip	3	As many as possible;	3–4
		more than 10, add weight	3–4
Pec deck	3	8	3–4
Triceps head caver	3	8	3–4
Triceps push-down	3	8	3–4
Big Dead Workout			
Deadlift	5	5	5–6
Straight-leg deadlift	3	8	3–4
Lateral pull-down	3	8	3–4
Dumbbell row	3	8	3–4
Biceps barbell curl	3	8	3–4
Biceps dumbbell curl	3	8	3–4

(continued)

Table 11.1 *(continued)*

	Sets	Reps	Rest (min)
Killer Combo Day			
Bench press	3	6	5
Lateral pull-down	3	6	5
Military press	3	6	5
Squat	3	6	5
Lunge	3	6	5
Leg curl	3	6	5
Upper-Body Day			
Dumbbell bench press	3	6	5
Inclined bench press	3	6	5
Pull-up	3	6	5
Cable row	3	6	5
Upright row	3	6	5
Military press	3	6	5
Lower-Body Day			
Squat	3	6	5
Lunge	3	6	5
Step-up	3	6	5
Leg extension	3	6	5
Leg curl	3	6	5
Calf raise	3	6	5

STRENGTH-SPEED WORKOUTS

The tempo for these workouts (table 11.2) should be slightly faster than the strength workouts. In the free-weight exercises, the eccentric portion of the movement should be controlled at two to three seconds. Movements should be performed explosively even though the resistance will prevent maximal speed. Resistance for these exercises should be lighter than that of the strength workout.

Table 11.2   Strength-Speed Workouts

	Sets	Reps	Rest (min)	Notes
Strength Jump and Push				
Box jump	4	6	3–4	As high as possible
Jump and reach	4	6	3–4	As high as possible
Long jump	4	6	3–4	As far as possible
High-pull snatch	3	6	5	
Push jerk	3	6	5	
Squat jumps	3	6	5	
Strength Rotate and Push				
Ancient log toss	3	6	3–4	Heavy medicine ball
Side toss	3	6	3–4	Heavy medicine ball
Overhead spike	3	6	3–4	Heavy medicine ball
Explosive band bench	3	6	4–5	
Push press	3	6	4–5	
Clean and jerk	3	6	4–5	
Strength Jump and Pull				
Lateral box push-off jump	3	6	3–4	With barbell
Linear box push-off jump	3	6	3–4	With barbell
Power clean	3	6	4–5	
Clean high-pull	3	6	4–5	
Walking lunge	3	6	4–5	
Strength Run				
Sled sprint forward	4	15 yds	3–4	Heavy weight

(continued)

Table 11.2 (continued)

	Sets	Reps	Rest (min)	Notes
Sled sprint lateral	4	15 yds	3–4	Heavy weight
Sled sprint backward	4	15 yds	3–4	Heavy weight
Clean	3	6	4–5	
Snatch high-pull	3	6	4–5	
Squat	3	6	4–5	
Strength Combo				
Medicine ball power drop	3	6	3–4	Heavy weight
Explosive band bench	3	6	3–4	Heavy weight
Plyometric push-up	3	6	3–4	
Push press	3	6	3–4	
Lateral pull-down	3	6	3–4	
Cable row	3	6	3–4	
Strength Rotational				
Side toss middle	3	6	3–4	Heavy weight
Side toss high	3	6	3–4	Heavy weight
Side toss low	3	6	3–4	Heavy weight
Seated side toss	3	6	3–4	Heavy weight
Reverse seated toss	3	6	3–4	Heavy weight
Two-hand hammer throw	3	6	3–4	
Strength Jump				
Lateral box push-off jump	3	6	3–4	Heavy weight
Linear box push-off jump	3	6	3–4	Heavy weight
Long jump with medicine ball	3	6	3–4	Heavy weight
Squat jump	3	6	3–4	Heavy weight
Walking lunge	3	6	3–4	Heavy weight

1 yd = .91 m

POWER WORKOUTS

The tempo for these workouts (table 11.3) should be as explosive as possible. Resistance is your body weight for jumping and push-up type exercises and moderate weight objects (balls) for rotational movements. Notice in explosive movements that exercises can concentrate on both speed and height or distance. When going for maximal distance or height, it may take an additional second or two to regain balance between repetitions. For upper-body throw-type movements, you may want to use multiple balls for release moves to keep the tempo up or throw against a wall so the ball returns back to you.

Table 11.3 Power Workouts

	Sets	Reps	Rest (min)
Jump and Throw Workout			
Jump and reach	3	6	5
Tuck jump	3	6	5
Split jump	3	6	5
Drop push-ups	3	6	5
Overhead spike throw	3	6	5
Reverse side toss	3	6	5
Jump and Rotate Workout			
Ancient log toss	4	6	5
Side toss	3	6	5
Axe chop	3	6	5
Hurdles forward for height	4	6	5
Hurdles lateral for height	3	6	5
Hurdles back for height	3	6	5
Plyometric Power Workout 1			
Drop push-ups	4	6	5
Plyo push-ups	3	6	5
Overhead spike throw	4	6	5
Lateral box push-off jumps	4	6	5
Linear box push-off jumps	4	6	5
Linear box step-ups for speed	3	6	5

(continued)

Table 11.3 *(continued)*

	Sets	Reps	Rest (min)
Power Combo Workout 1			
Jump and reach	4	6	5
Long jump	3	6	5
Backward hurdle jump	3	6	5
Split jumps for speed	3	8	5
Medicine ball drop chest push	4	8	5
Side toss for speed	3	8	5
Killer Power Workout*			
Single-leg tuck jump	3	6	5**
Single-leg lateral hurdle	3	6	5**
Single-leg forward hurdle	3	6	5**
Single-arm chest pass	3	6	5**
Axe chops	4	8	5**
Power Combo Workout 2			
Speed skaters for distance	4	6 per leg	4
90-degree hurdle jumps	4	6	5
180-degree hurdle jumps	3	6	5
Plyometric push-ups	4	6	5
Side toss	4	6	4
Ancient log toss	3	6	4

*No rest between alternate leg or arm.
**Between same leg and arm.

SPEED-STRENGTH WORKOUTS

The tempo for these workouts (table 11.4) should be as fast as possible. The resistance for these workouts is body weight, but unlike the power workouts, the athlete moves forward, backward, and laterally. These workouts are probably the most common means of improving speed and power for most sports. Movements should attempt to work skills as well as improve coordination, balance, and acceleration. The agility drills should be distance-limited by sport (meaning the total length should be within a court or field's dimension) and have anywhere from two to five direction changes.

Table 11.4 Speed-Strength Workouts

	Sets	Reps	Rest (min)
Ladder Sprint Workout			
Agility ladder forward	4–5	8–10	3–4
Agility ladder lateral	4–5	8–10	3–4
Agility ladder backward	4–5	8–10	3–4
Overspeed bungee sprint	5	20 yds	3–4
Overspeed bungee lateral	5	20 yds	4
Overspeed bungee backward	5	20 yds	4
Sprint Agility Workout			
Resisted running forward	5	20 yds	4
Resisted running lateral	5	20 yds	4
Resisted running backward	5	20 yds	4
Pro-agility	4–5	20 yds	3–4
M drill	4–5	20 yds	3–4
Basic box drill	4–5	20 yds	3–4
Speed Sprint Workout			
Speed skaters for speed	3	8 per leg	4
Pro-agility	6	20 yds	4
Line hops	3	8	3
Parachute forward	5	20 yds	3–4
Parachute backward	5	20 yds	3–4
Parachute zig zag	5	20 yds	3–4
Speed Ladder Workout			
Acceleration sprints—15 yards	3	8	3–4
Backward sprints—15 yards	3	8	4
Split jumps for speed	3	8	4
Agility ladder icky	4–5	8–10	3–4
Agility ladder boxer	4–5	8–10	3–4
Agility ladder buzz saw	4–5	8–10	3–4

(continued)

Table 11.4 *(continued)*

	Sets	Reps	Rest (min)
Agility Hill Workout			
L drill	4–5	20 yds	3–4
N drill	4–5	20 yds	3–4
Arrow drill	4–5	20 yds	3–4
Hill sprint forward	4	15 yds	4
Hill sprint lateral	4	15 yds	4
Hill sprint backward	4	15 yds	4
Linear Speed Workout			
Resisted running forward	4	15 yds	4
Overspeed running forward	4	15 yds	4
Hill sprints forward	4	15 yds	4
Hurdles forward for speed	4	15 yds	4
Hurdles lateral for speed	4	8	4
Lateral Speed Workout			
Resisted running lateral	4	15 yds	4
Overspeed running lateral	4	15 yds	4
Hill sprints lateral	4	15 yds	4
Hurdles for speed lateral hops	4	8	4
Hurdles sidestep	4	8	4

1 yd = .91 m

PURE-SPEED WORKOUTS

These workouts (table 11.5) are reserved for the few sports that truly need pure-speed development. Since most sports require the body to move, these workouts will be used sparingly or in combination with other workouts. By its name, speed is the key. Resistance, where applicable, should be very light with implements not being more than three or four pounds (1.36 or 1.81 kilograms). If the resistance becomes too great, speed will decrease, losing the intended effect of the workout. When using resistive tubing, band thickness (strength) should be in accordance with the strength of the athlete to allow speed movements. There are fewer workouts, but combinations of each can make an unlimited number of exercises.

Table 11.5 Pure-Speed Workouts

	Sets	Reps	Rest (min)	Notes
Speed Tube Training				
Speed squats	3	8	2–3	As fast as possible
Hip flexion	3	8	2–3	As fast as possible
Hip extension	3	8	2–3	As fast as possible
Leg curls	3	8	2–3	As fast as possible
Leg extension	3	8	2–3	As fast as possible
Chest press/push-ups	3	8	2–3	As fast as possible
Standing rows	3	8	2–3	As fast as possible
Overhead press	3	8	2–3	As fast as possible
Biceps curls	3	8	2–3	As fast as possible
Triceps extension	3	8	2–3	As fast as possible
Twisting abdominal crunches	3	8	2–3	As fast as possible
Rotational Speed Workout				
Ancient log toss	3	8–10	2–3	1–4lbs against wall fast
Side toss	3	8–10	2–3	1–4lbs against wall fast
Axe chop	3	8–10	2–3	1–4lbs against wall fast
Rotational tubing up/down	3	10–12	2–3	As fast as possible
Rotational tubing side middle	3	10–12	2–3	As fast as possible
Rotational tubing side low	3	10–12	2–3	As fast as possible
Rotational tubing side high	3	10–12	2–3	As fast as possible
Rope Sprint Workout				
Rope ball axe chop	3	8–10	2–3	1–4lbs against wall fast
Rope ball log toss	3	8–10	2–3	1–4lbs against wall fast
Rope ball hammer throw	3	8–10	2–3	1–4lbs against wall fast
Rope ball one-arm punch	3	8–10	2–3	1–4lbs against wall fast
Bike sprints	10	10 seconds	2–3	As fast as possible
¼ or ½ eagle turns	5	20 seconds	2–3	As fast as possible

The above workouts are similar to any combination weight training workouts. Each rep should be as explosive as possible. Any of these exercises can be done in combination with other workouts or split into specific body parts.

1 lb = .45 g

INDEX

Note: Italicized *f* or *ff* following page numbers indicate a figure or figures on that page, respectfully. Italicized *t* or *tt* following page numbers indicate a table or tables on that page, respectfully.

ABOUT THE AUTHOR

David Sandler, MS, CSCS*D, CCS, HFD, is an exercise science and strength and conditioning professor at Florida International University, where he developed and currently directs the strength and conditioning curriculum. He is a doctoral candidate and former strength and conditioning coach for the University of Miami. He has presented more than 50 international, national, and regional lectures and published 15 scientific abstracts and more than 30 articles in power and strength training. Sandler has been a strength and conditioning consultant for more than 15 years and is currently a co-owner of StrengthPro, a South Florida-based strength and conditioning consulting company. He is the Chairman for The Arnold Strength Training Summit and enjoys faculty and developmental positions with several organizations. Sandler also serves on the advisory board for *Muscle and Fitness* magazine.